Cobourg Ontario Book 2 in Colour Photos, Saving Our History One Photo at a Time

Photography
by Barbara Raué
©2019

Series Name: Cruising Ontario

Book 226: Cobourg Book 2

Cover photo: 320 College Street, Page 26

Series Name: Cruising Ontario
Saving Our History One Photo at a Time
in colour photos

Books Available in Alphabetical Order:
Aberfoyle, Acton, Ajax, Alton, Amherstburg, Ancaster, Arthur, Auburn, Aylmer, Ayr, Beaver Valley, Belgrave, Belleville, Bloomingdale, Blyth, Brantford, Brockville, Burford, Burlington, Caledon, Caledonia, Cambridge, Carlow, Chatsworth, Clifford, Collingwood, Conestogo, Delhi, Dorchester to Aylmer, Drayton, Drumbo, Dundas, Dunlop, Eden Mills, Elmira, Elora, Erin, Essex, Fergus, Goderich, Grimsby, Guelph, Hagersville, Hamilton, Hanover, Harriston, Hespeler, Jarvis, Kingston, Kingsville, Kitchener, Lake Superior, Lincoln, Linwood, Listowel, London, Lucknow, Merrickville, Mono, Mount Forest, Mount Pleasant, Neustadt, New Hamburg, Newboro, Newport, Niagara-on-the-Lake, Niagara Falls, North Bay, Oakville, Onondaga, Orangeville, Orillia, Oshawa, Owen Sound, Palmerston, Paris, Pelham, Perth, Peterborough, Petrolia, Pickering, Port Colborne, Port Elgin, Portland, Preston, Rockwood, Sarnia, Sault Ste. Marie, Seaforth, Sheffield, Shelburne, Simcoe, Smiths Falls, Smithville, Southampton, St. Catharines, St. George, St. Jacobs, St. Marys, St. Thomas, Stoney Creek, Stratford, Thamesford, Thunder Bay, Tillsonburg, Toronto, Waterdown, Waterford, Waterloo, Welland, Wellesley, West Flamborough, Westport, Whitby, Windsor, Wingham, Woodstock

Book 212-215 Haldimand County

Book 216: Sudbury

Book 217: Parry Sound

Book 218-219: Uxbridge

Book 220: Port Perry

Book 221-222: Stouffville

Book 223: Colborne

Book 224: Grafton, Bolton

Book 225-230: Cobourg

Table of Contents

Cobourg is a town in Southern Ontario ninety-five kilometers (59 miles) east of Toronto and 62 kilometers (39 miles) east of Oshawa. It is located along Highway 401. To the south, Cobourg borders Lake Ontario.

The settlements that make up today's Cobourg were founded by United Empire Loyalists in 1798. Settlers started arriving in Cobourg in the 1790s when at the time it was known for its forty houses, two inns, four stores, several distilleries, a grist mill and about 350 people. The Town was originally a group of smaller villages such as Amherst and Hardscrabble, which were later named Hamilton. In 1808 it became the district town for the Newcastle District. It was renamed Cobourg in 1818, in recognition of the marriage of Princess Charlotte Augusta of Wales to Prince Leopold of Saxe-Coburg-Saalfeld (who later become King of Belgium).

James Cockburn, born in England, moved to Montreal with his family in 1832. In 1845 he came to Cobourg to practice law and, until 1849, shared a practice with D'Arcy Boulton, another prominent politician. Married in 1854 to Isabella Susan Patterson, Cockburn began raising a family and found interest in public affairs. He was elected to the Cobourg town council in 1856, 1858 and 1859. During this time, when plans for Victoria Hall floundered due to lack of finances, Cockburn offered the leadership which saw the project completed in 1860. While serving in local politics Cockburn acquired a reputation for honesty, fair dealing, integrity and sound logic. He was one of the Fathers of Confederation.

Cobourg retains its small-town atmosphere, in part due to the downtown and surrounding residential area's status as a Heritage Conservation District.

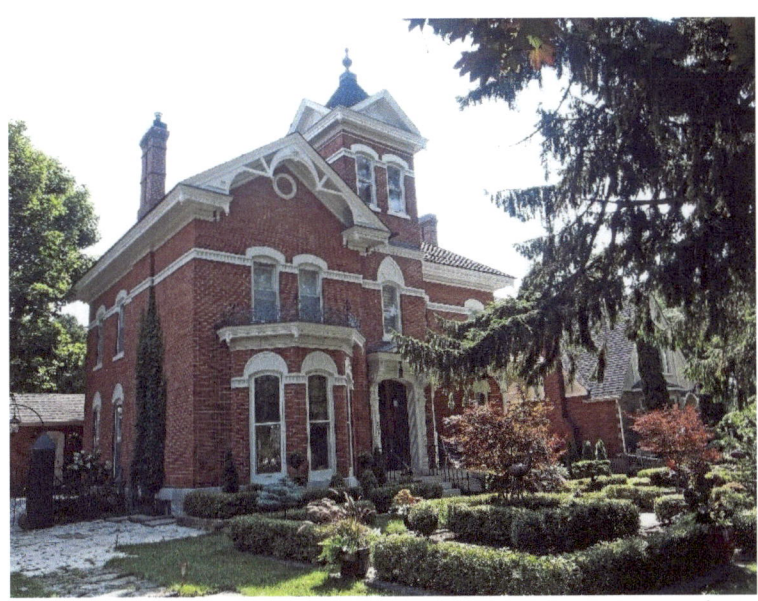

202 Church Street – 1878 – The Mulholland and McArthur House - Italianate Villa style – built by Robert Mulholland – asymmetrical 'L' plan with a short square tower crowned by an iron urn; at the base of the tower is a paneled doorway. The beaded string course, ornate roof cornice, pediments and iron cresting above the bay window, and barge board on the eave emphasize the sense of gaiety. The pale red bricks of the house are complimented by white arched window and door moldings.

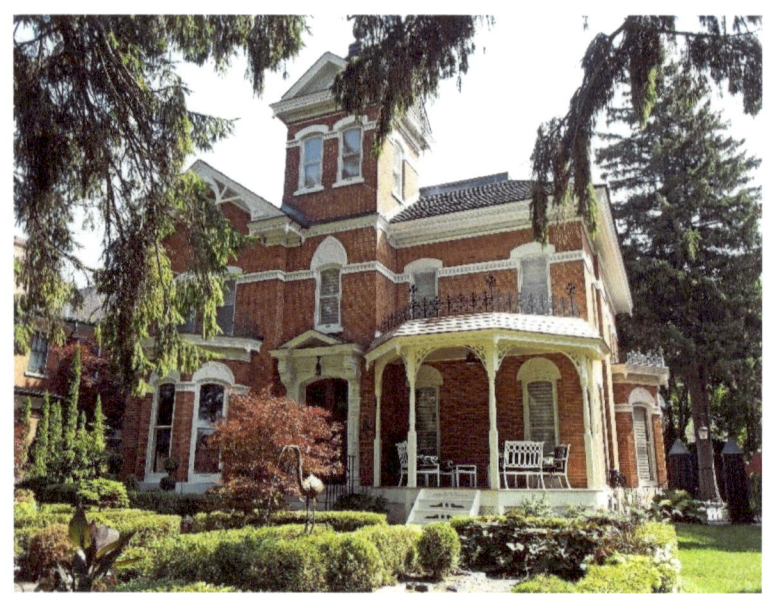

202 Church Street

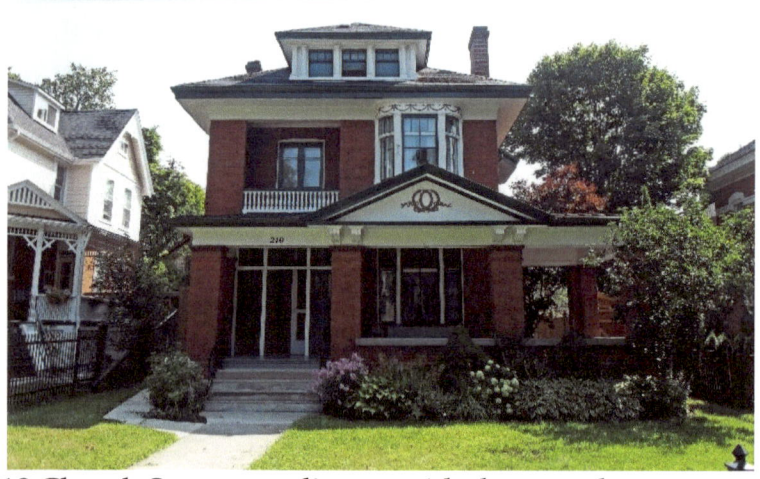

210 Church Street – pediment with decorated tympanum, second-floor balcony and bay window, dormer in attic

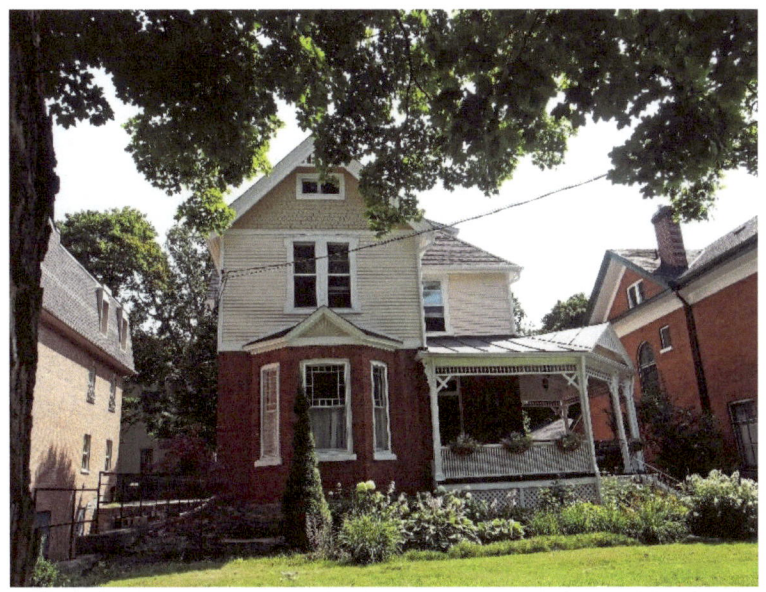

216 Church Street – 1898 - built by Harry Wicksteed in the Queen
Anne style; bay window

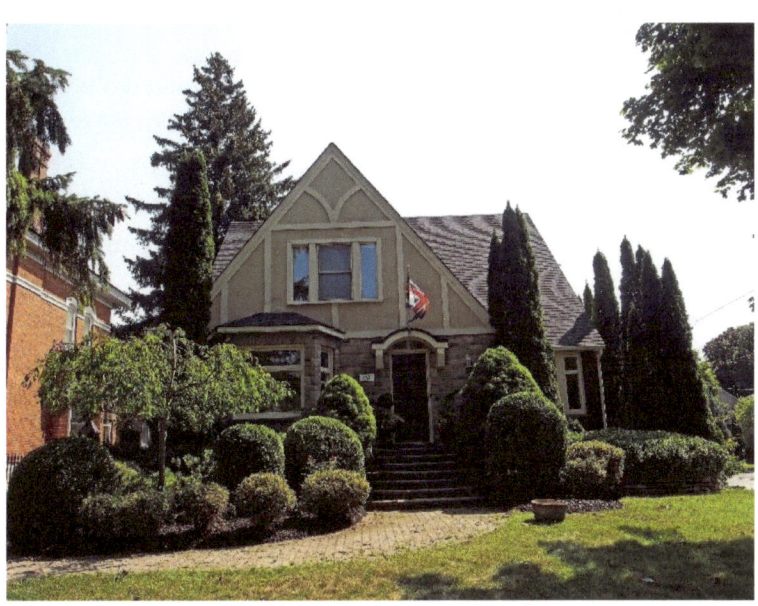

198 Church Street - Tudor

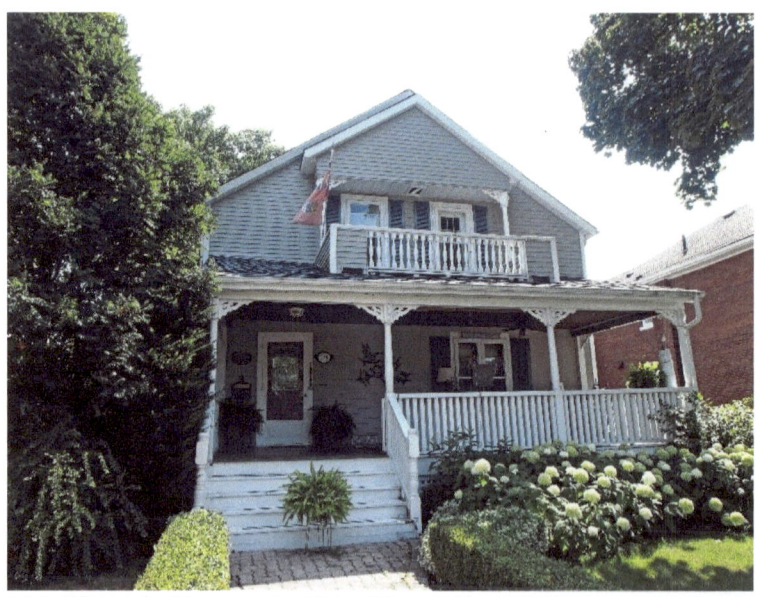

184 Church Street – 1888 – The Albert House – Victoria Cottage built by William Beer and rented to summer visitors. Two storeys, gable roof, the windows are two-over-two and double hung, aluminum siding. The veranda is the full front of the façade, has a shed roof, with balcony above.

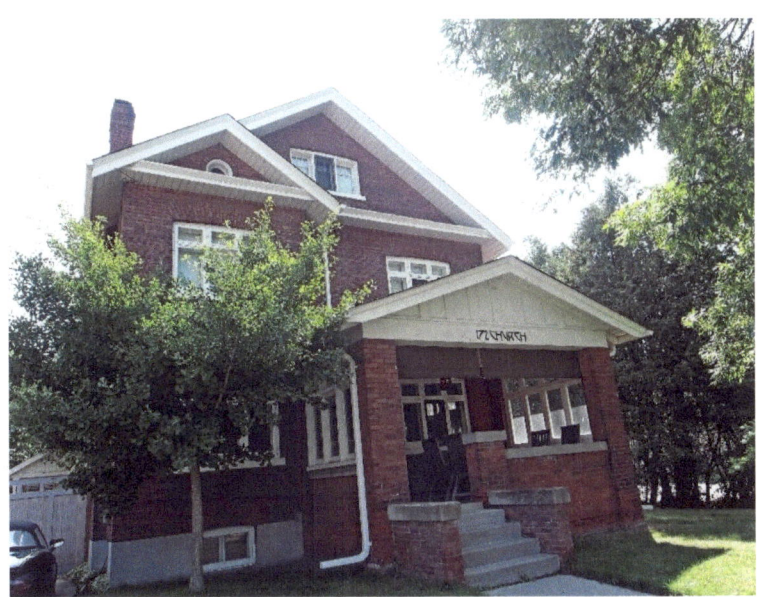

172 Church Street

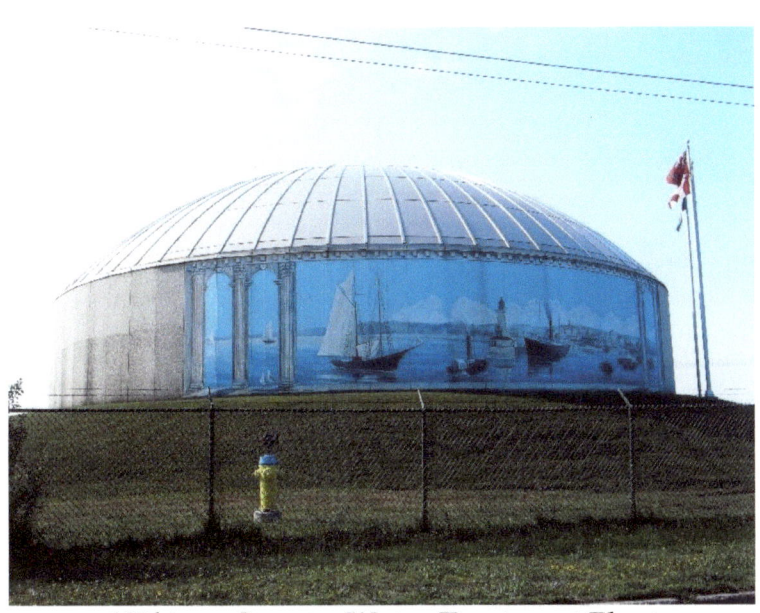

6 D'Arcy Street – Water Treatment Plant

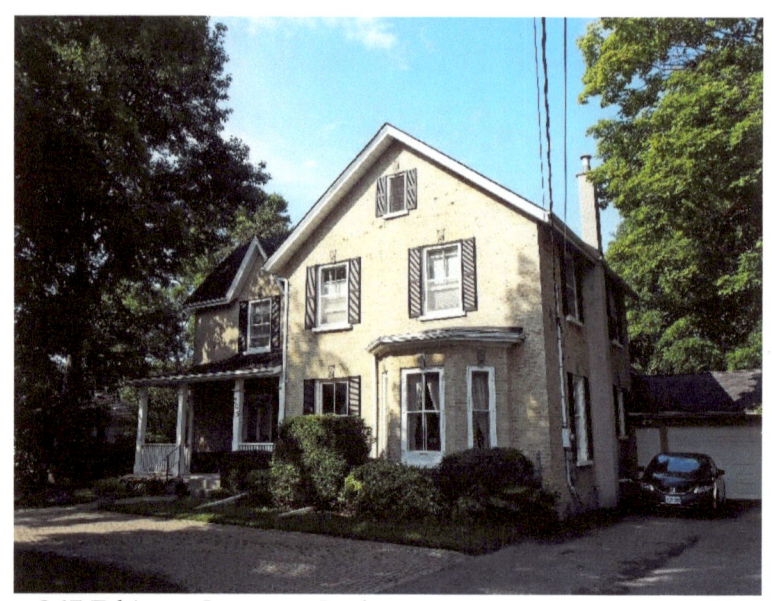

265 D'Arcy Street – Gothic – 1878-1880 - Alexander Macdonald House

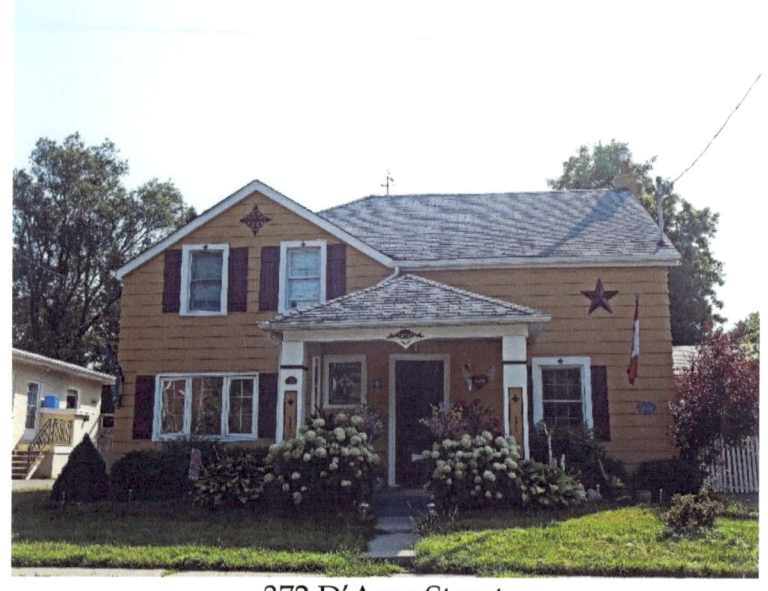

372 D'Arcy Street

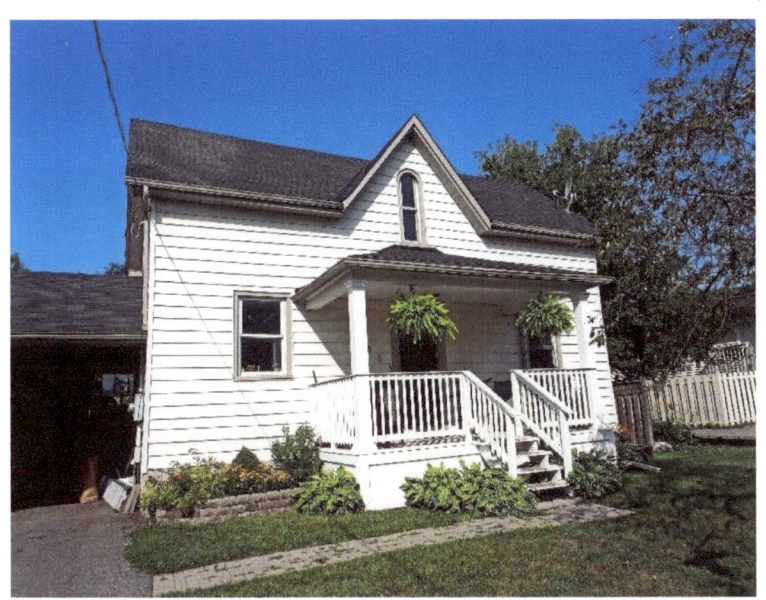

385 D'Arcy Street - Gothic

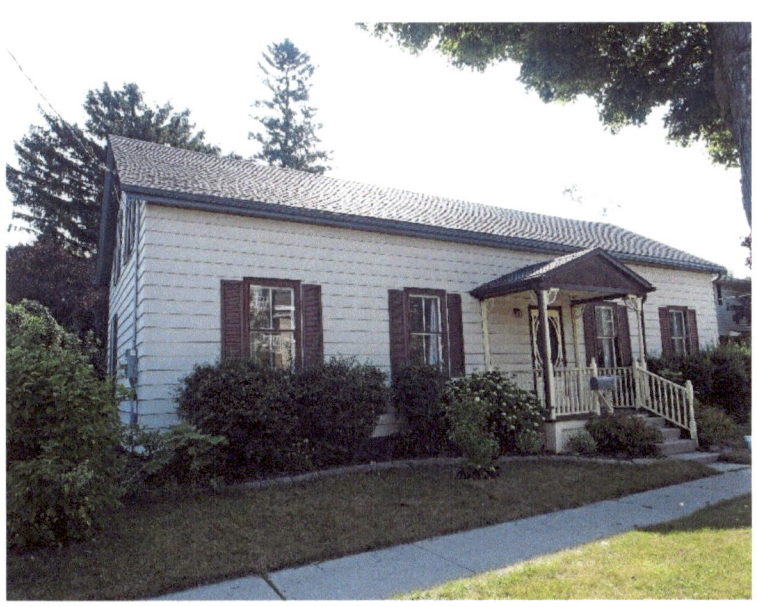

D'Arcy Street

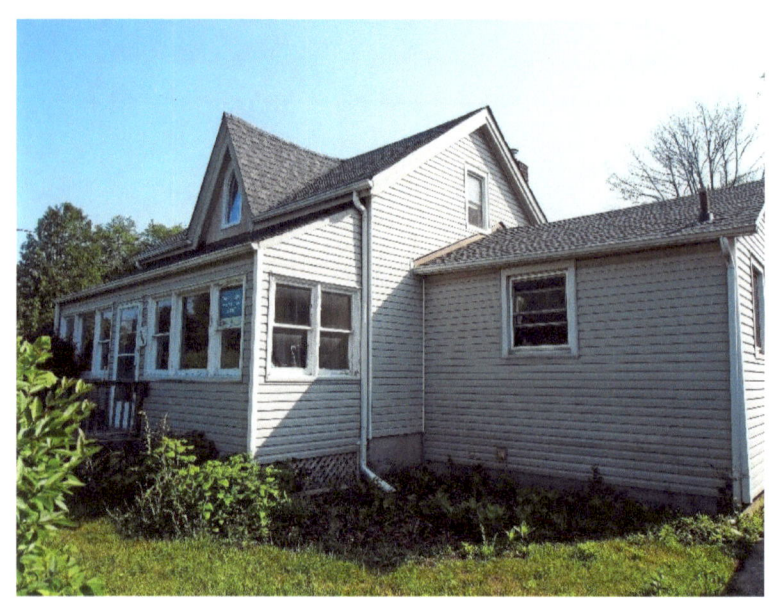

344 D'Arcy Street – c. 1840s - Gothic

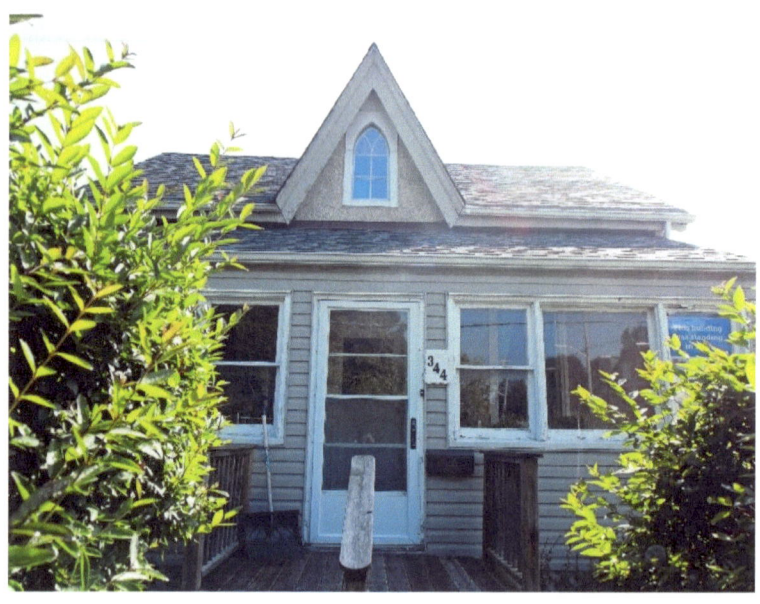

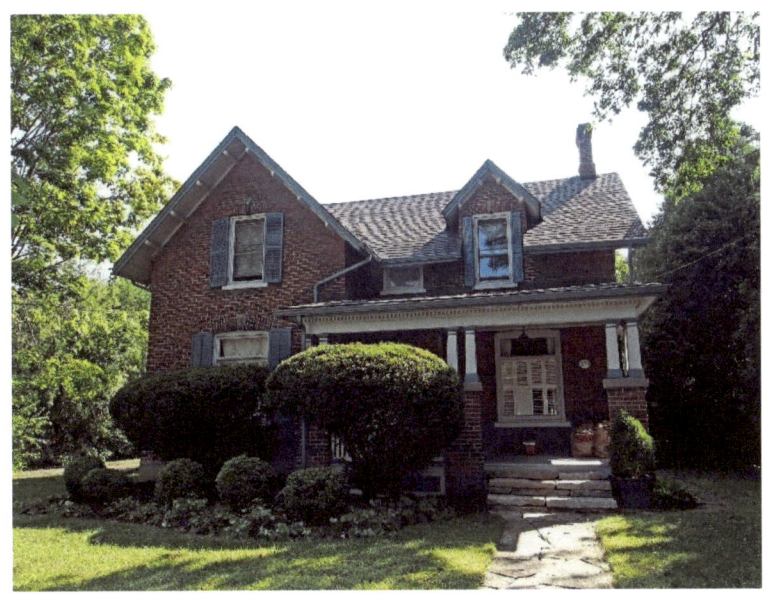

370 Walton Street – c. 1874

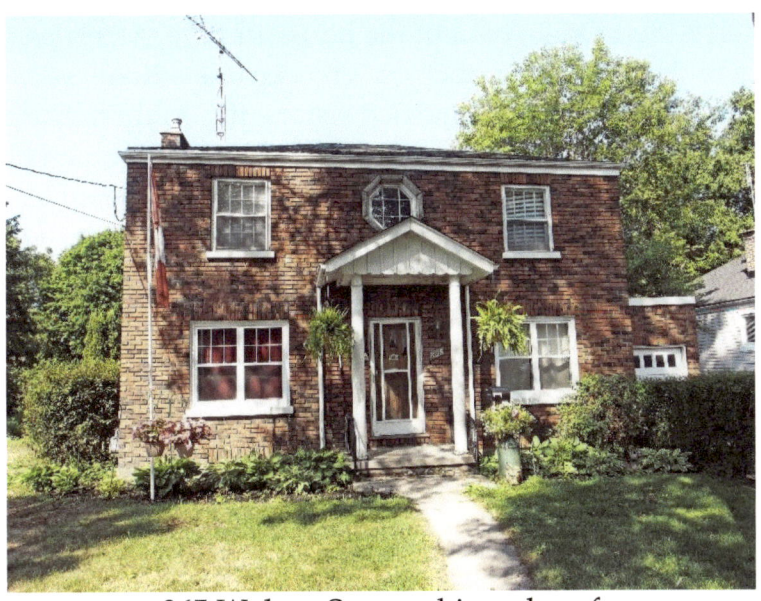

365 Walton Street – hipped roof

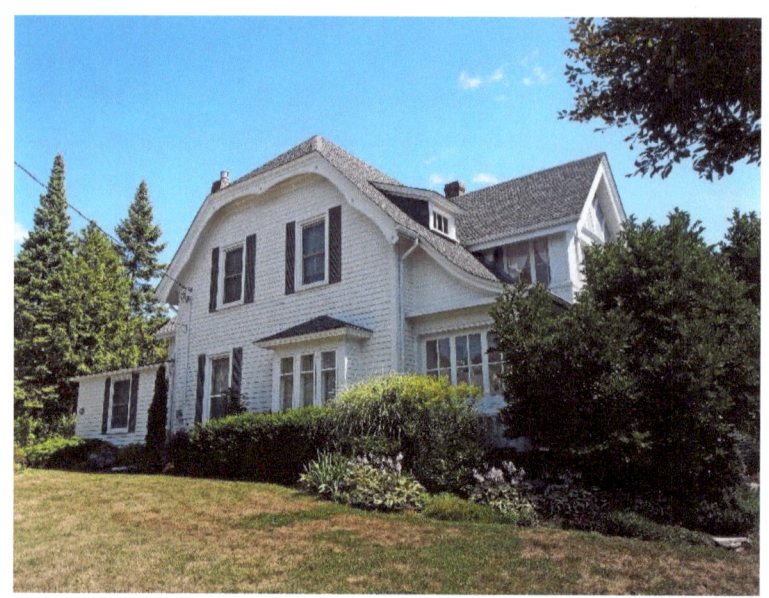

356 Walton Street – c. 1876 – 'Sunny Brae' was built by Nathaniel Burwash, a teacher at Victoria College who later became its president, in a Vernacular style. The front gable and porch, added circa 1905, gave it more charm. Another teacher, Albert Odell, bought the house in 1900. Albert and his brother John were both teachers who became school inspectors, and both had married sisters, the daughters of a local merchant. When Albert's wife died in 1904 John and his family moved in with his brother. When war broke out ten years later, John enlisted at the age of 48. He had been the commanding officer of the Cobourg Heavy Battery, a militia regiment, which became part of the 2nd Heavy Battery, Canadian Field Artillery, under Lieutenant-Colonel Odell's command. This battery arrived in France in September of 1915 and returned home in May of 1919.

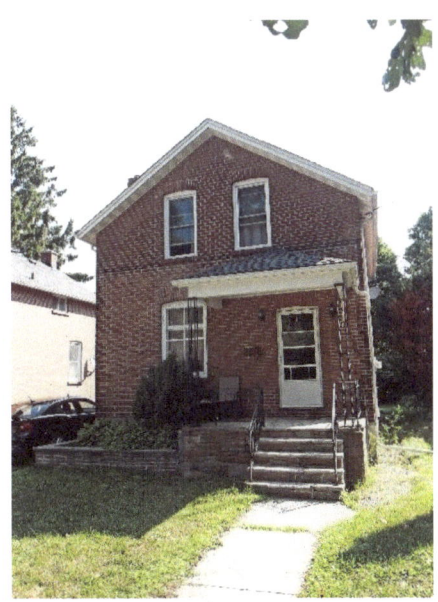

270 Walton Street

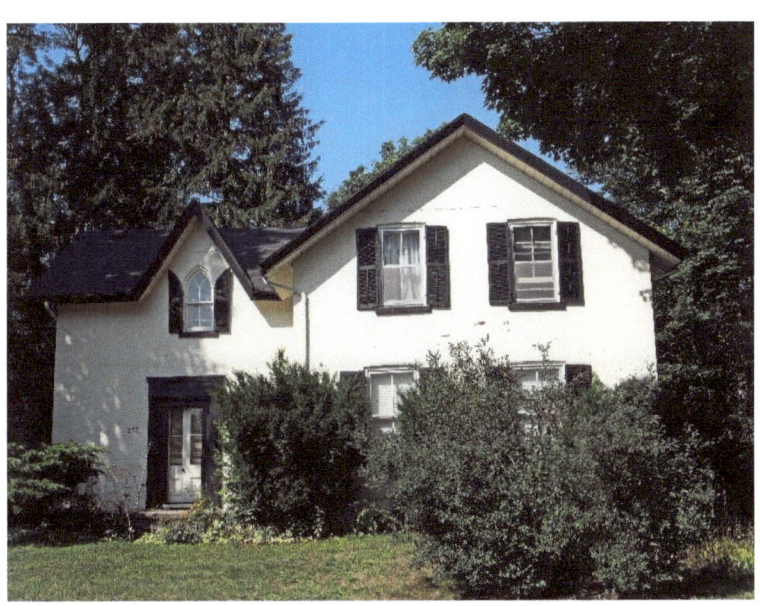

257 Walton Street - Gothic

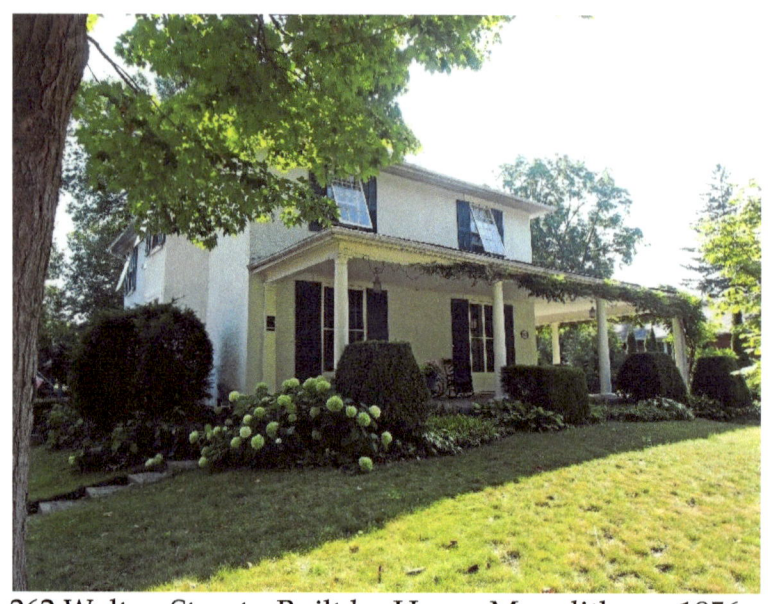

262 Walton Street - Built by Henry Meredith – c. 1856 – Regency Vernacular style. From about 1939 to 1974, residence home of A. Roy Willmott Q.C. of firm Willmott and Irvine who became Ontario's first Chief Judge in 1962.

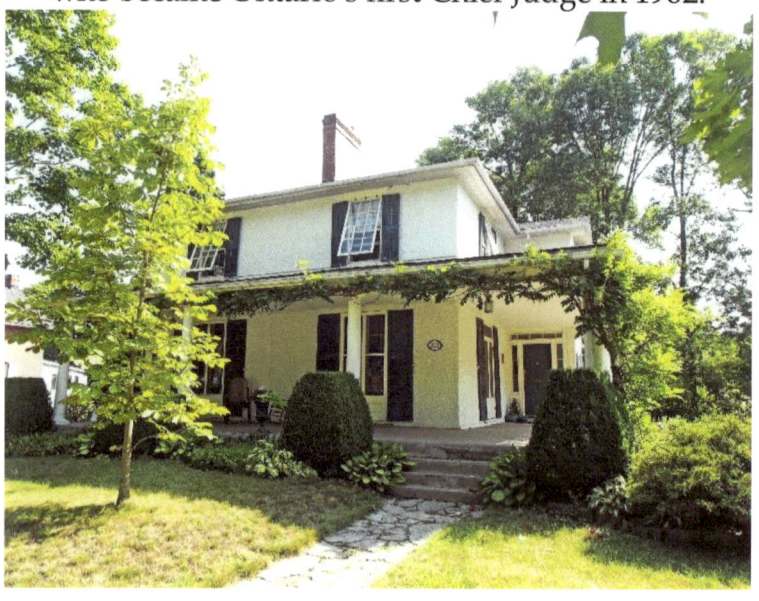

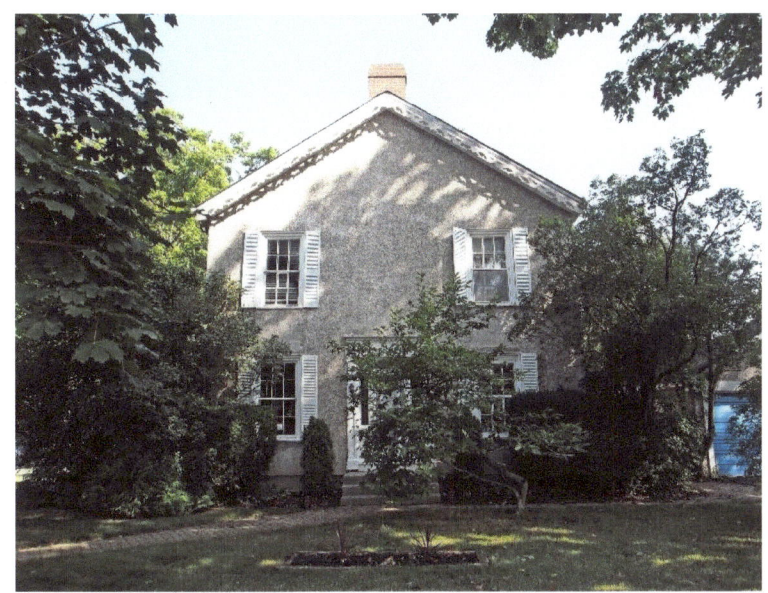

394 Henry Street – c. 1858

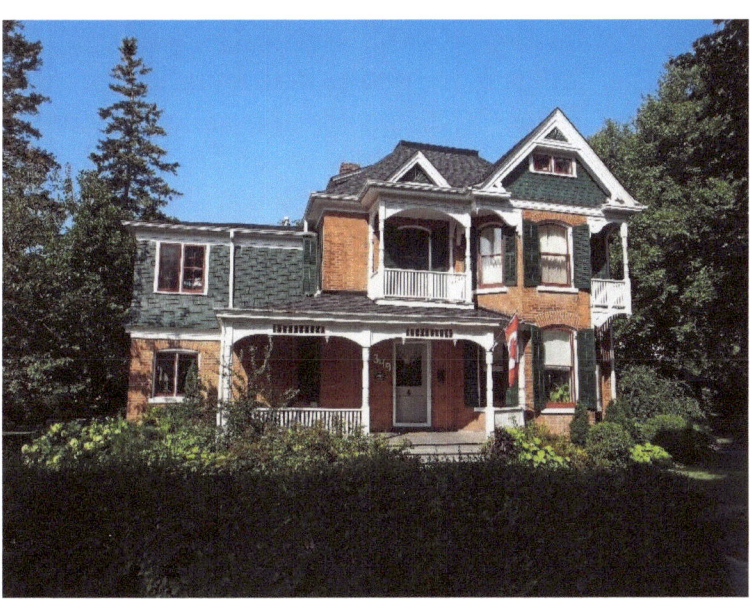

349 Henry Street – Kensington Cottage – c. 1880-1881

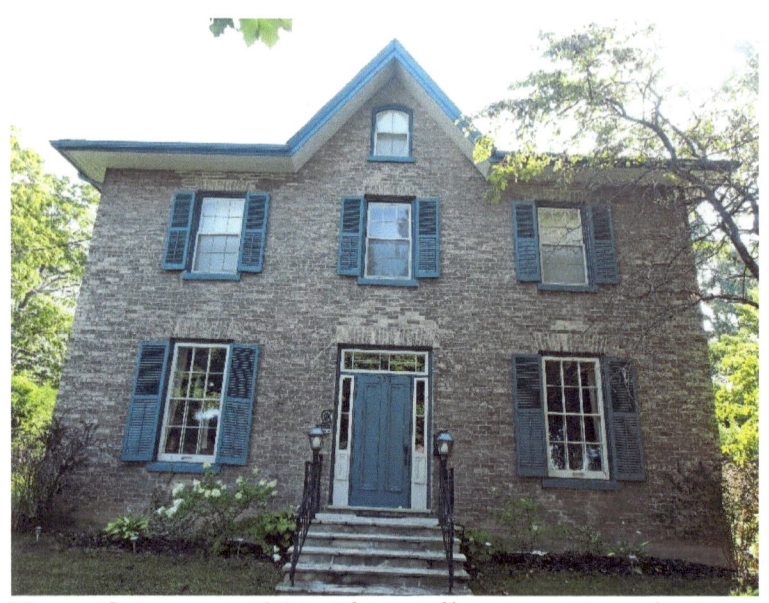

332 Henry Street – c. 1856 - This well -proportioned Victorian house shows Regency influence in its three-bay façade and hipped roof but also has a Gothic-style gable with an attic window. It was built for Andrew Hewson, an Irish immigrant who operated a successful dry goods and millinery store in town. He and his wife had six children, and their daughter, Charlotte, and her husband, Deputy-Sheriff David McNaughton, lived with them for many years. Their only son, Edmund Hewson McNaughton, was killed at Bully-Grenay, France, while serving with the Cobourg Heavy Battery. On August 9, 1918, an enemy shell hit a storage shed containing 9 artillery shells and 5 tons of cordite. A 9.2 Howitzer gun was destroyed and 26-year old McNaughton and two other Cobourg young men were killed.

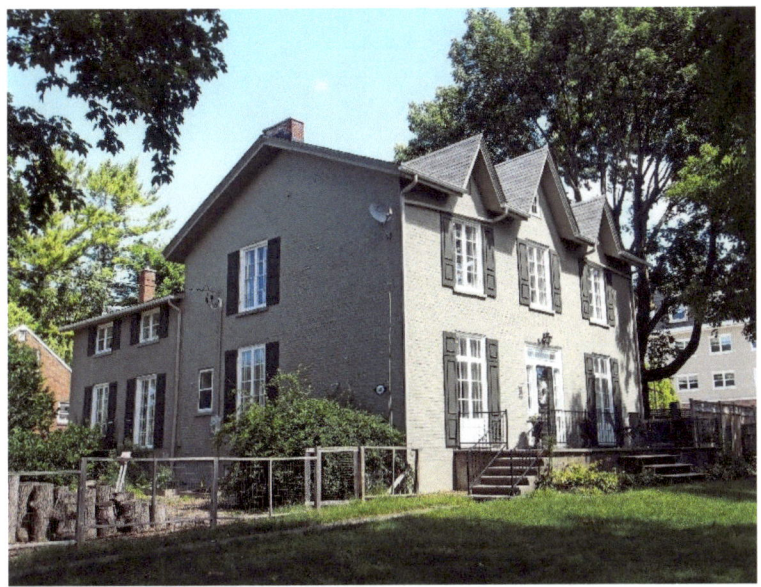

308 Henry Street – 1855 - Regency style, built by the Rev. Walton Beck, son-in-law of George Boulton. The three gables, each containing a Gothic window, were added in 1870.

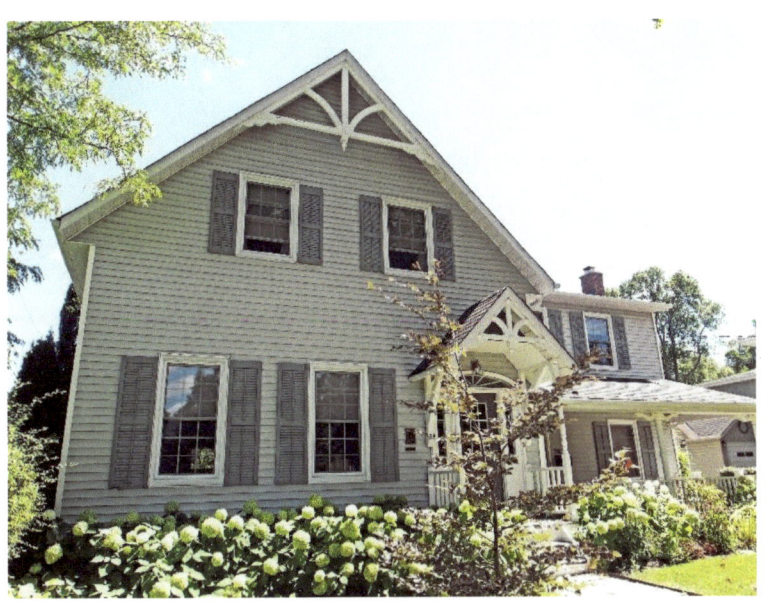

286 Henry Street – c. 1880s - Built by Edward Tinney, local carpenter, two storeys

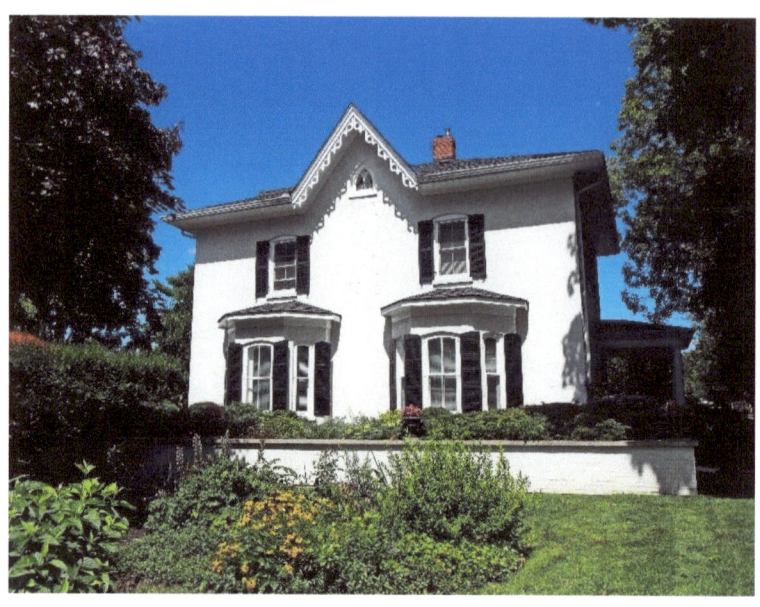

303 Henry Street – c. 1882 – Vernacular with Gothic elements – verge board trim, bay windows

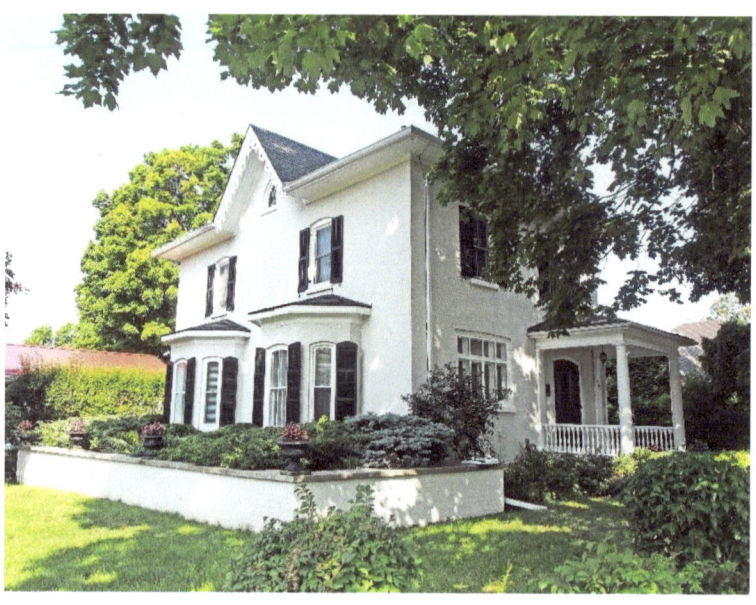

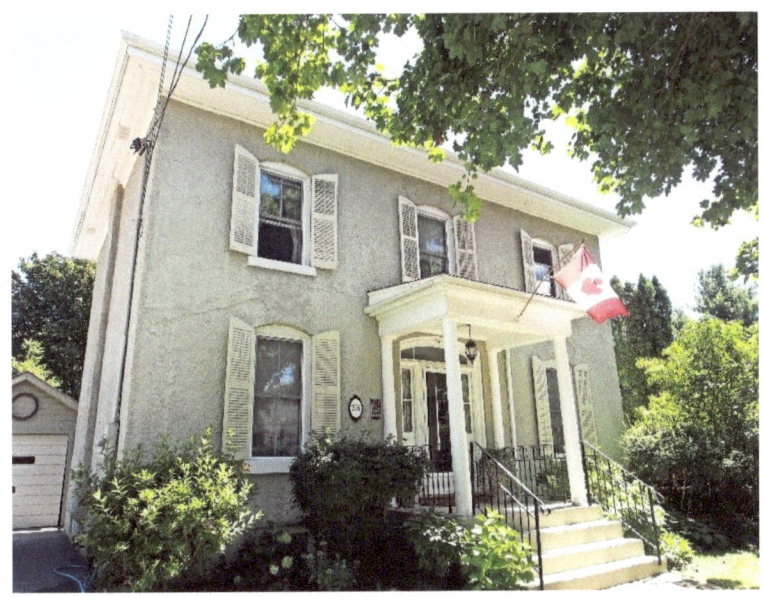

276 Henry Street – two-storey house

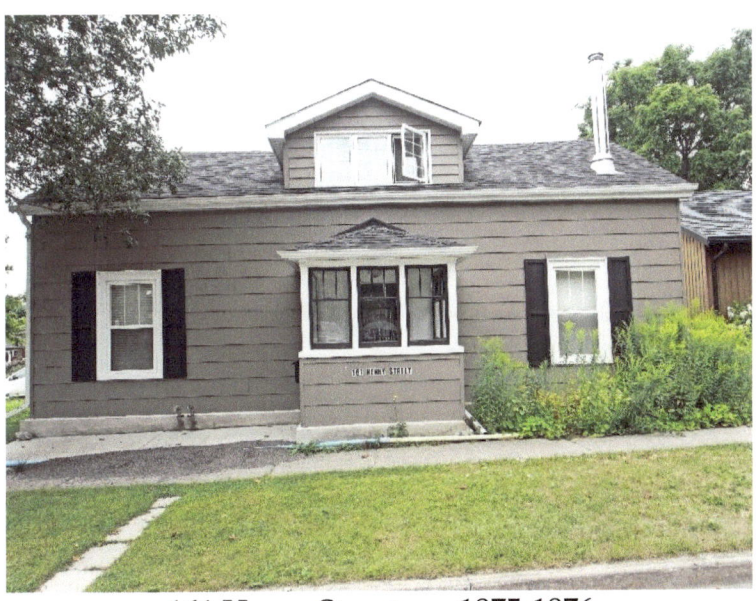

161 Henry Street – c. 1875-1876

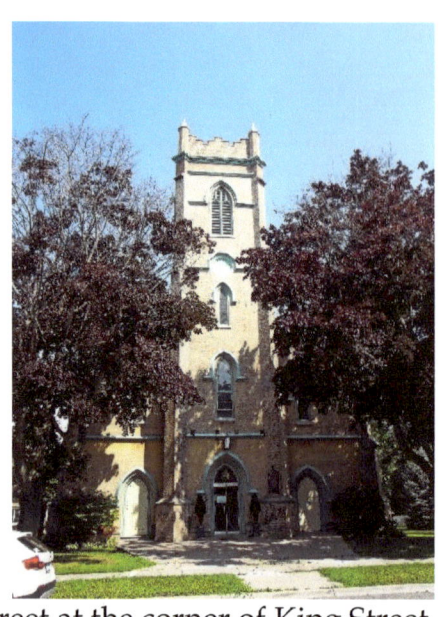

240 College Street at the corner of King Street - Church of St. Peter – Construction began in 1851, finished in 1854 – stepped battlements, early Gothic Revival style

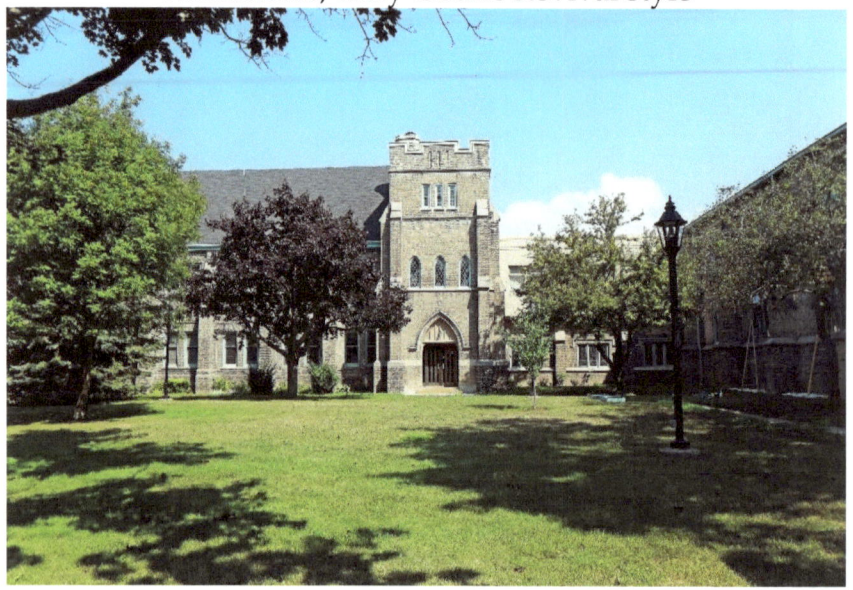

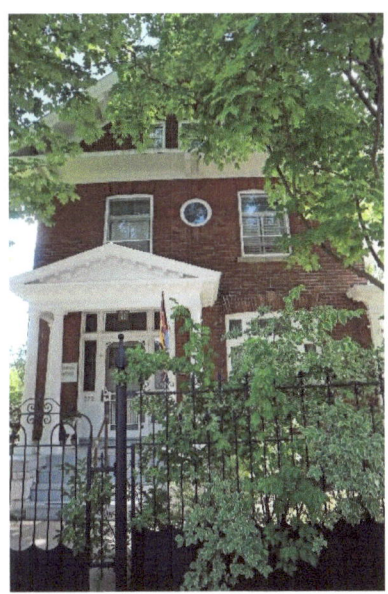

272 College Street – 1903 - This Edwardian style townhouse was built for Mary Cruso Buck, widow of Roe Buck, son of one of Cobourg's earliest settlers and tavern owner, Elijah Buck. Classic Revival portico

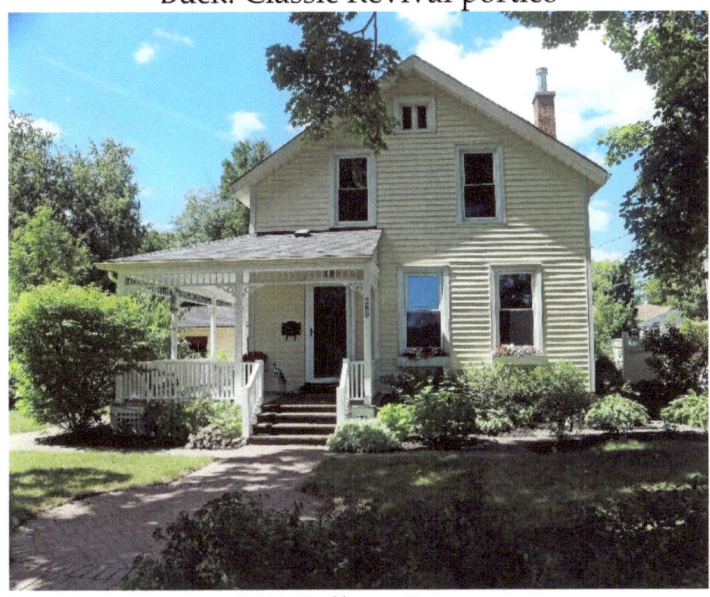

285 College Street

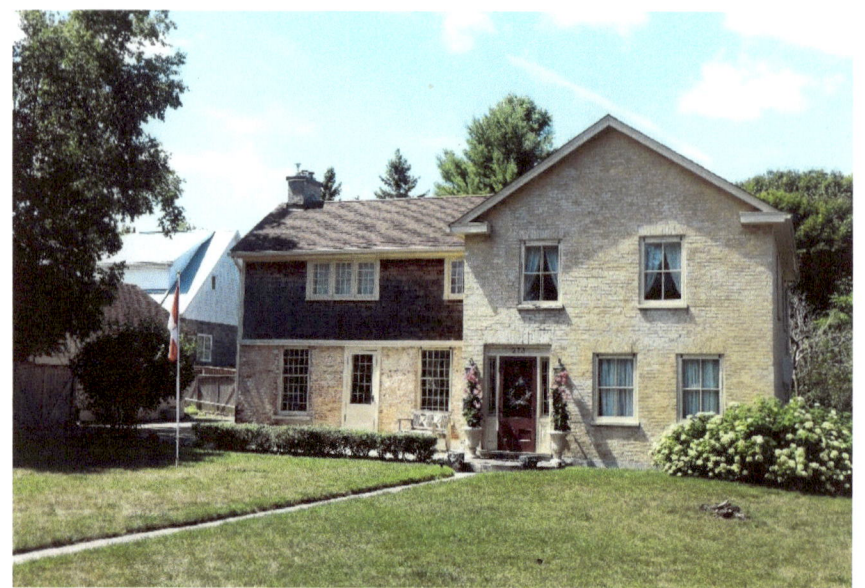

273 College Street – Matthew Hobart, a Cobourg cabinet maker, had this stucco house built about 1858 in the Classic Revival style. Sidelights, double-hung windows two up two down on the gabled façade, cornice return on gable

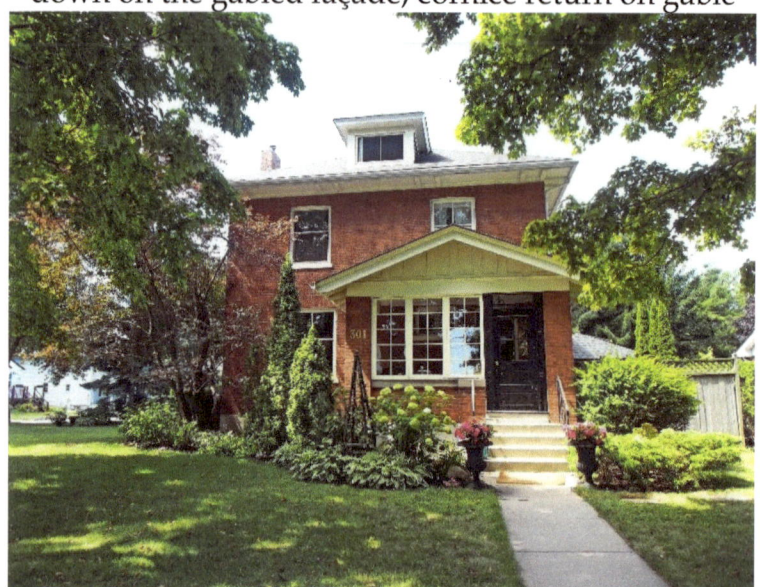

301 College Street – pediment, dormer

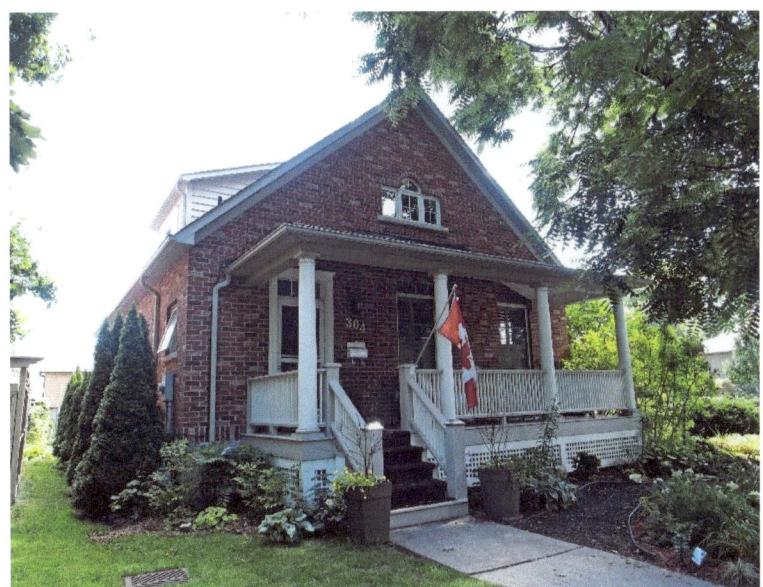

304 College Street

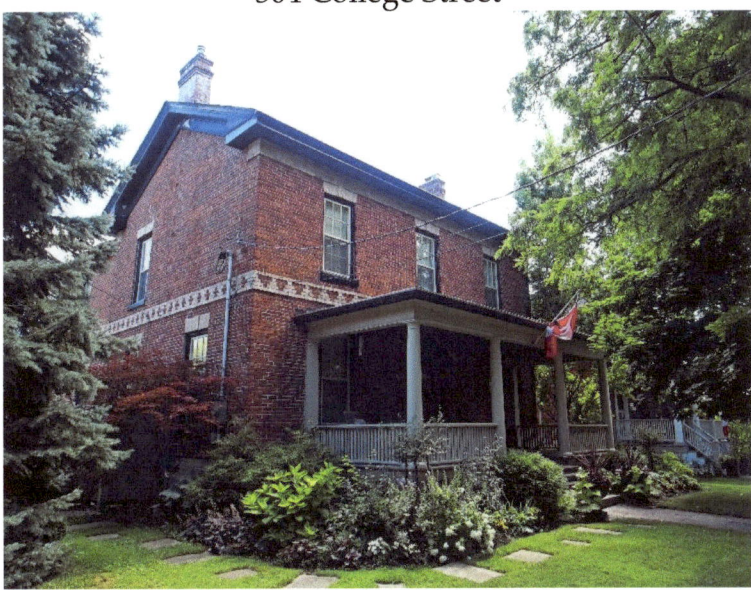

306 College Street – 1857 - The decorative pattern of two-colored brick work is the outstanding feature of this house, built in Georgian Loyalist style for a local merchant, Lazarus Payne. Members of the Payne family lived here for over seventy years.

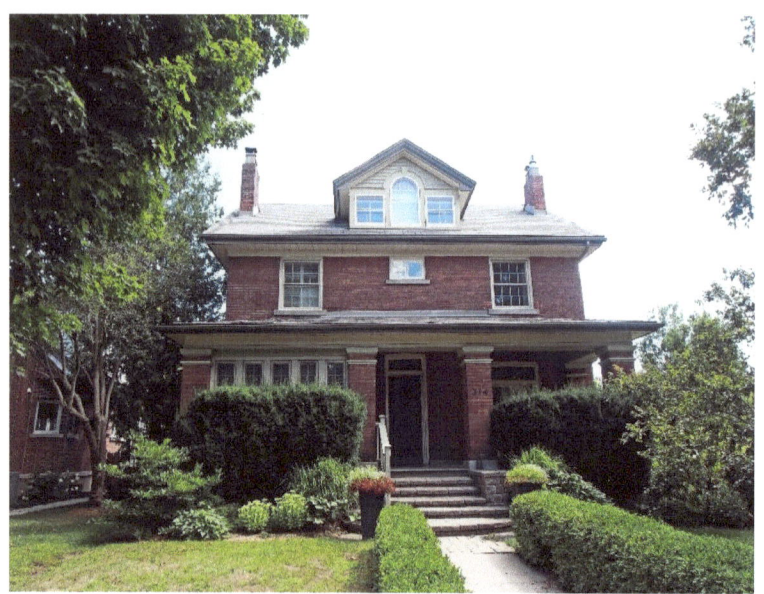

314 College Street – Palladian-type window in dormer

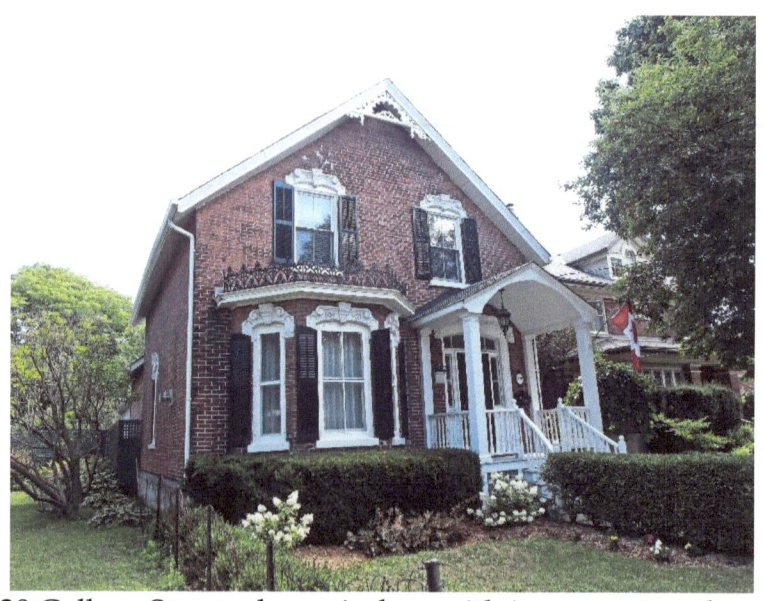

320 College Street – bay window with iron cresting above,
sidelights and transom windows

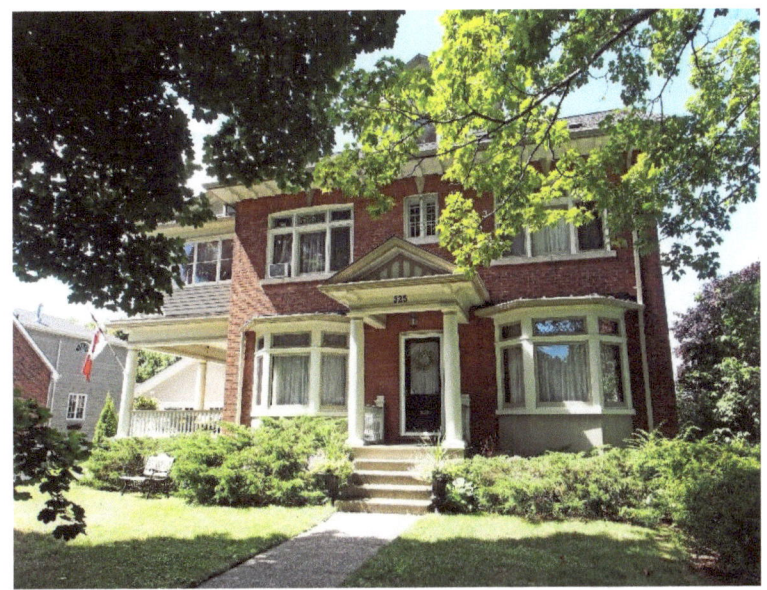

325 College Street – pediment, bay windows

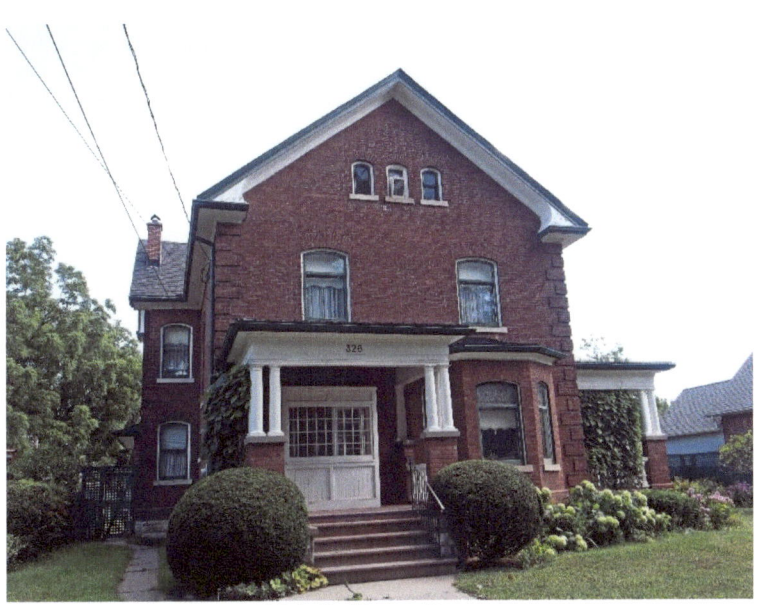

326 College Street

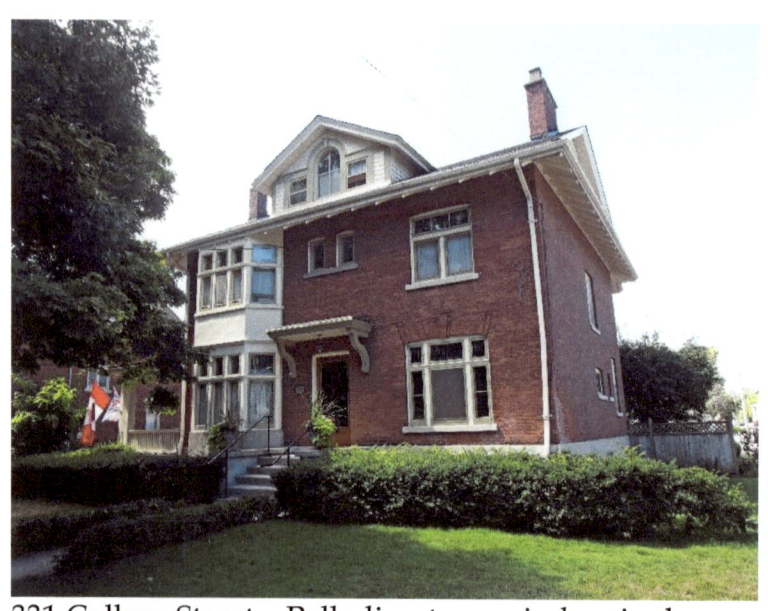

331 College Street – Palladian-type window in dormer

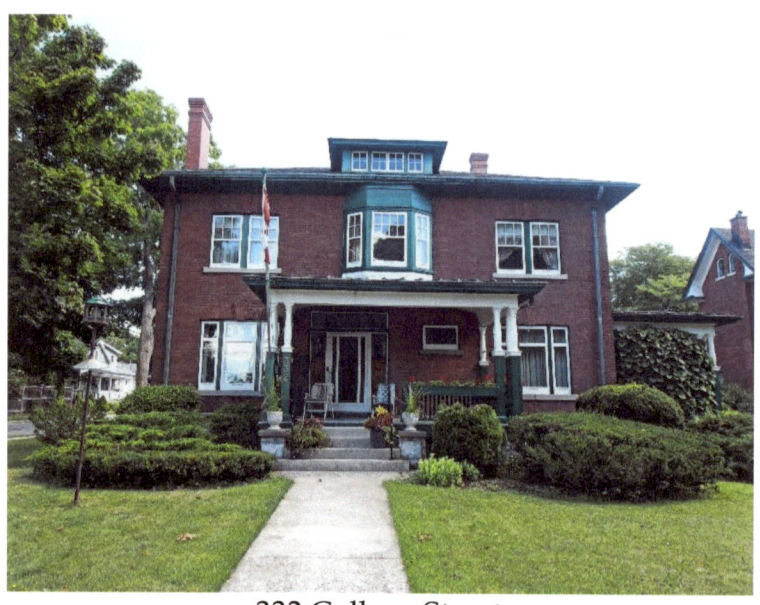

332 College Street

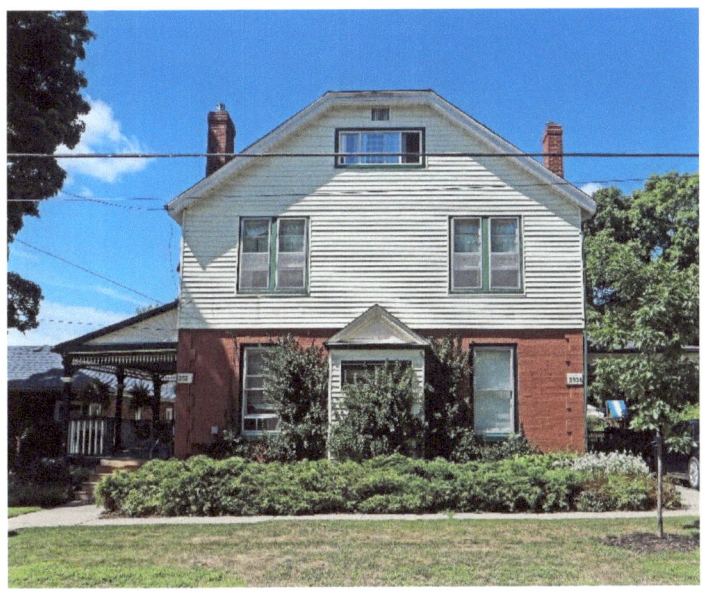

353 College Street – c. 1880s or 1890s – Doherty House - Vernacular, chipped gable, hip-roofed veranda supported by eight Doric columns, corner quoins, multi-paned casement window on top floor

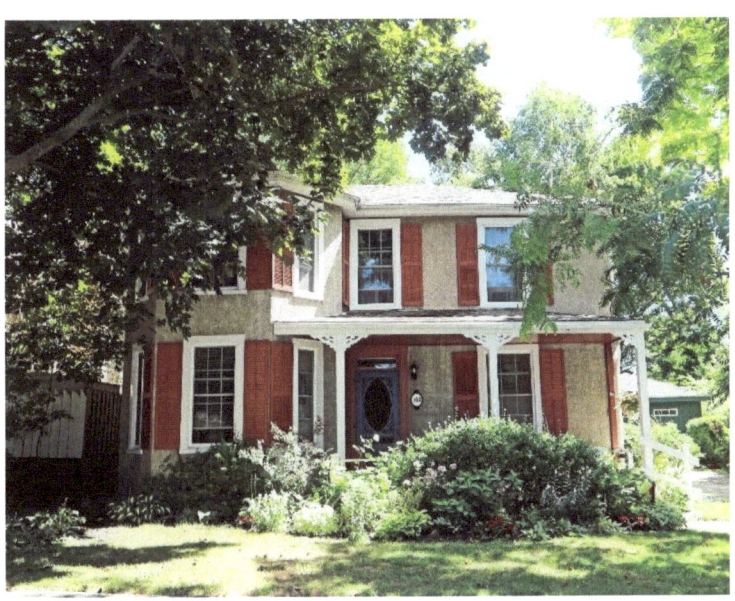

360 College Street - shutters

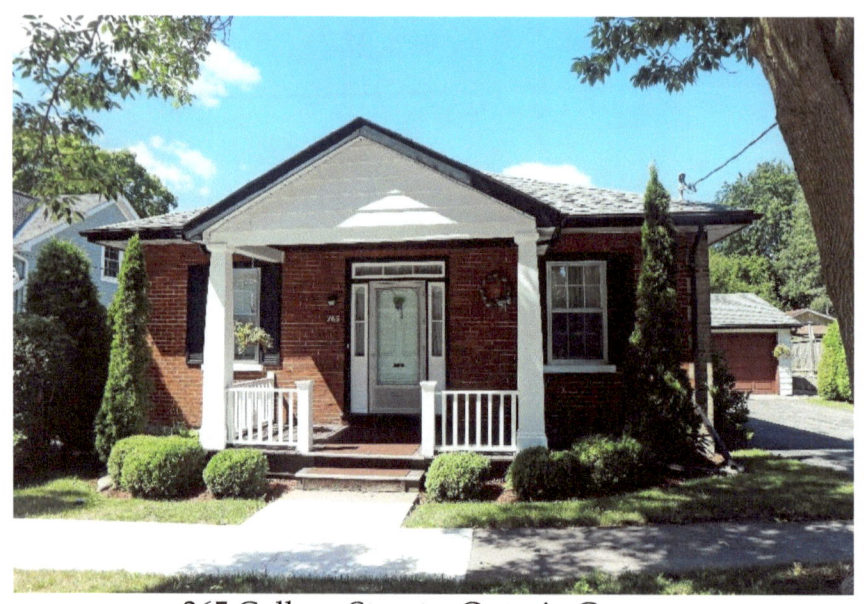

365 College Street – Ontario Cottage

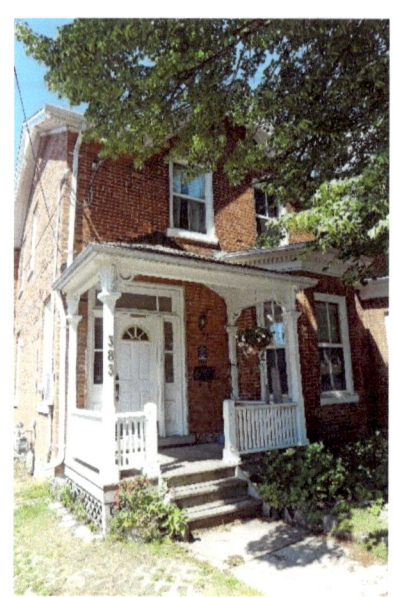

383 College Street – c. 1877 - late-Victorian row house

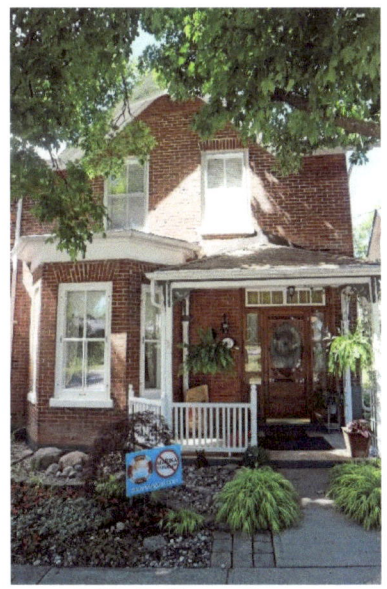

385 College Street

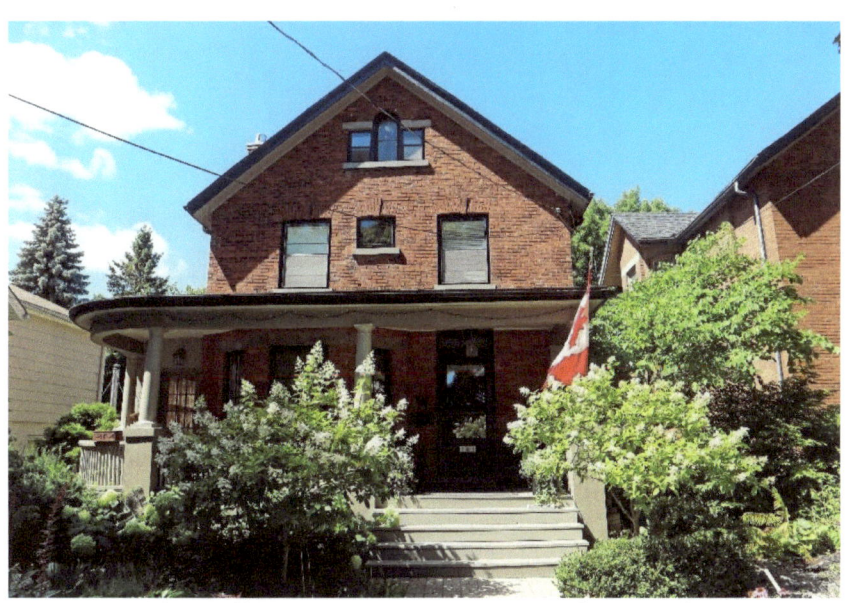

389 College Street – wraparound veranda

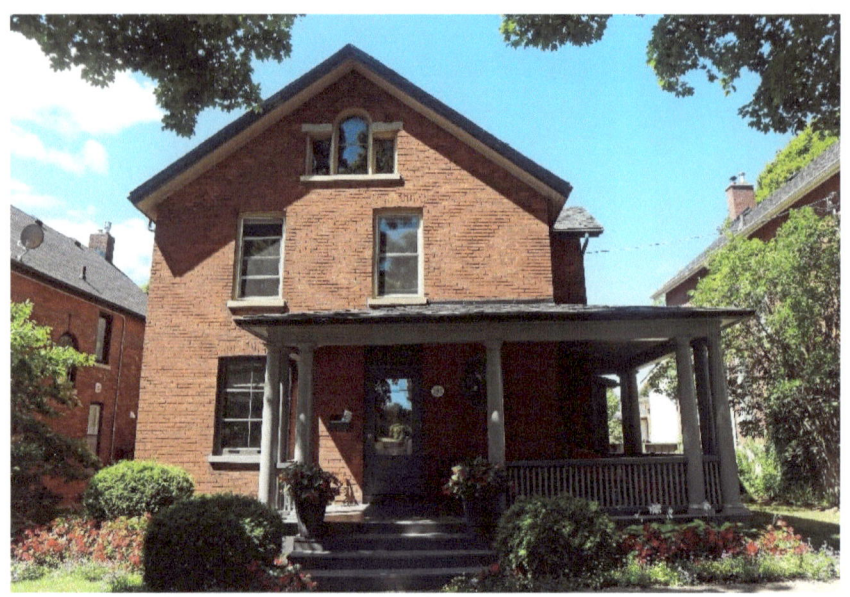

393 College Street – Palladian-type window in gable

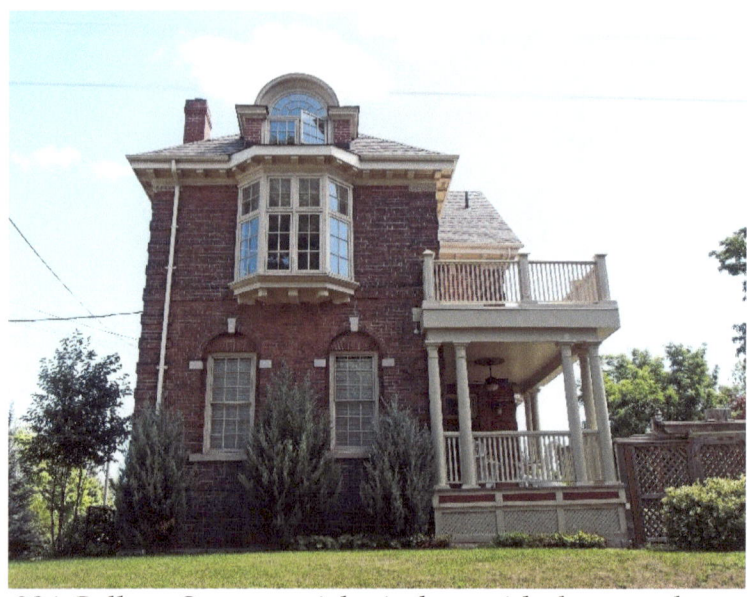

394 College Street – oriel window with dormer above

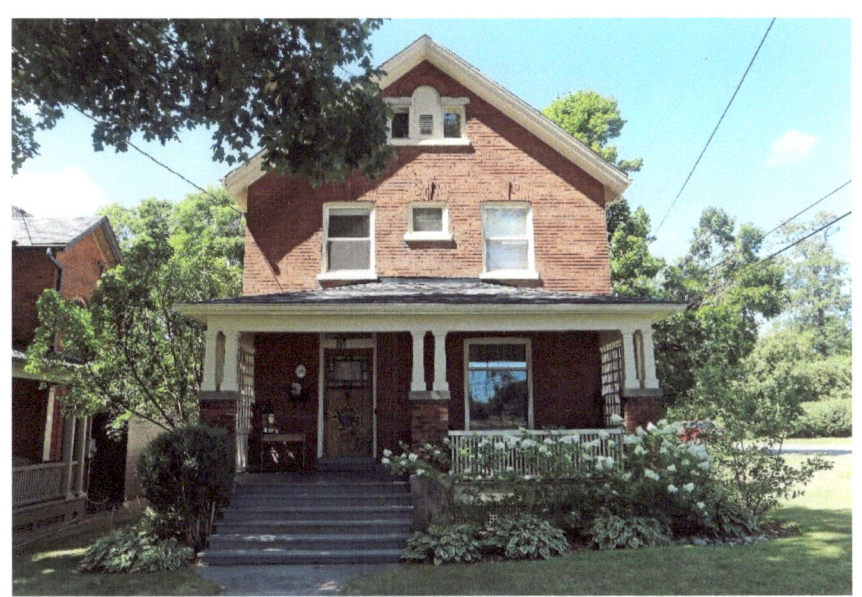

395 College Street

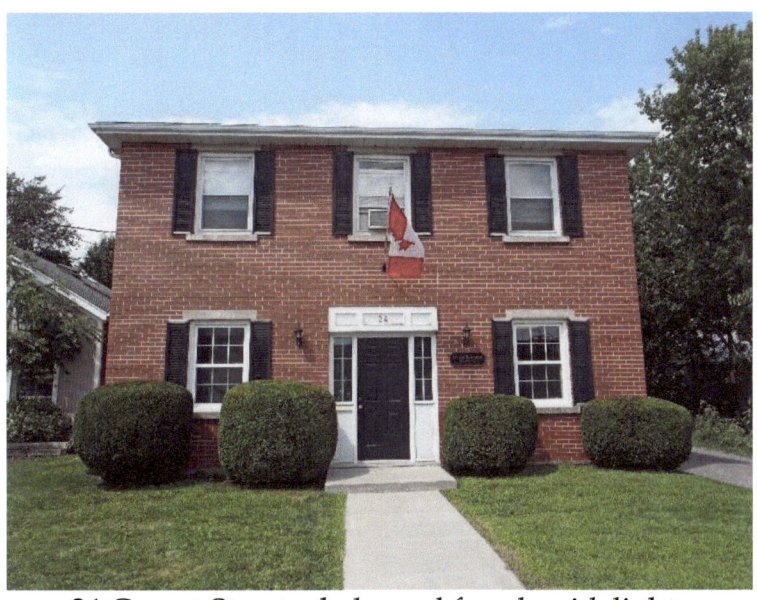

24 Covert Street – balanced façade, sidelights

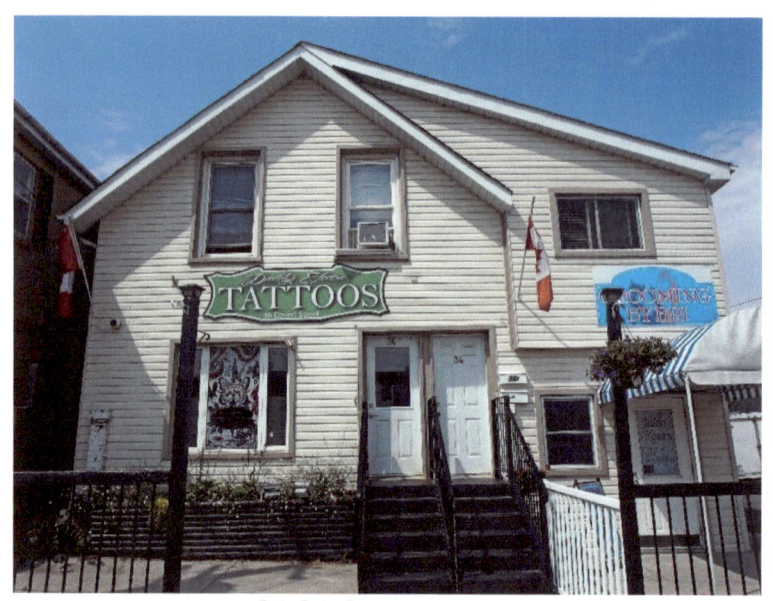

34-36 Covert Street

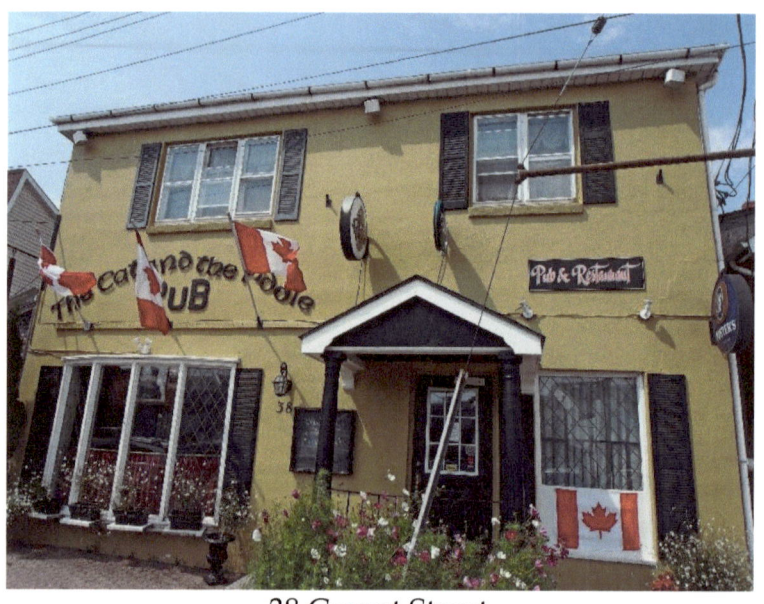

38 Covert Street

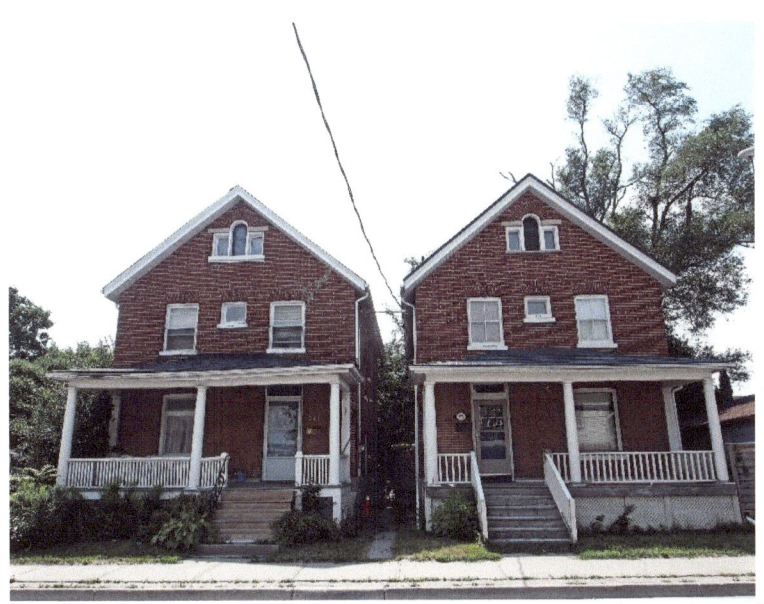

273 and 275 George Street – Palladian-type windows in gables

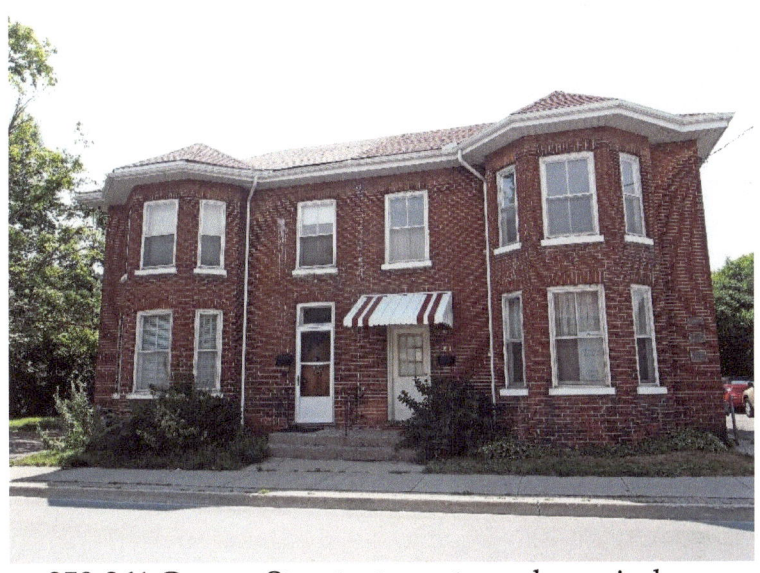

259-261 George Street – two-storey bay windows

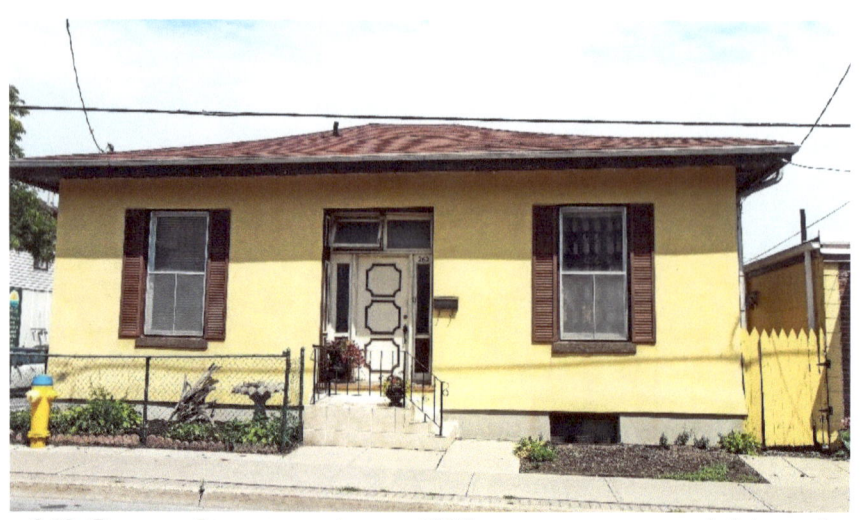

262 George Street – prior to 1858 – stucco covered, hipped roof, sidelights, transom

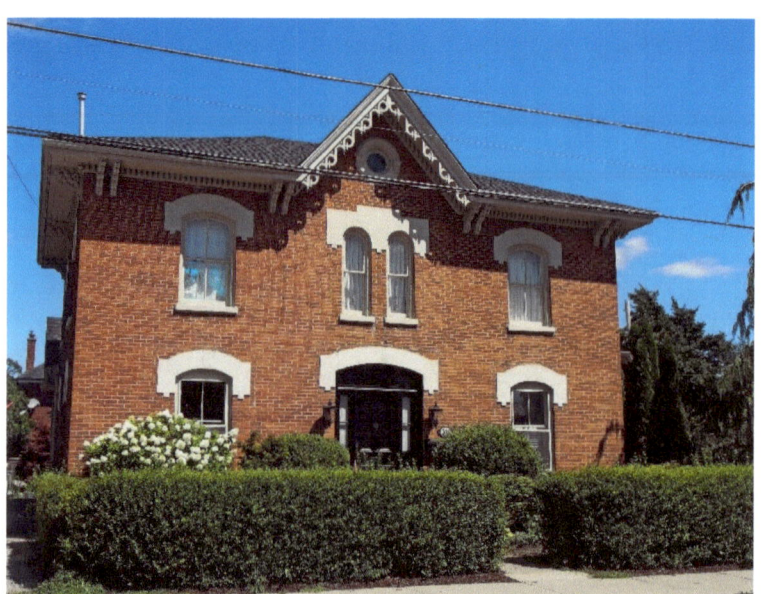

314 George Street – The MacNachtan Home – 1876 – red-brick Italianate house with contrasting window and door heads in buff brick, a circular window in the gable, paired cornice brackets, verge board trim on gable

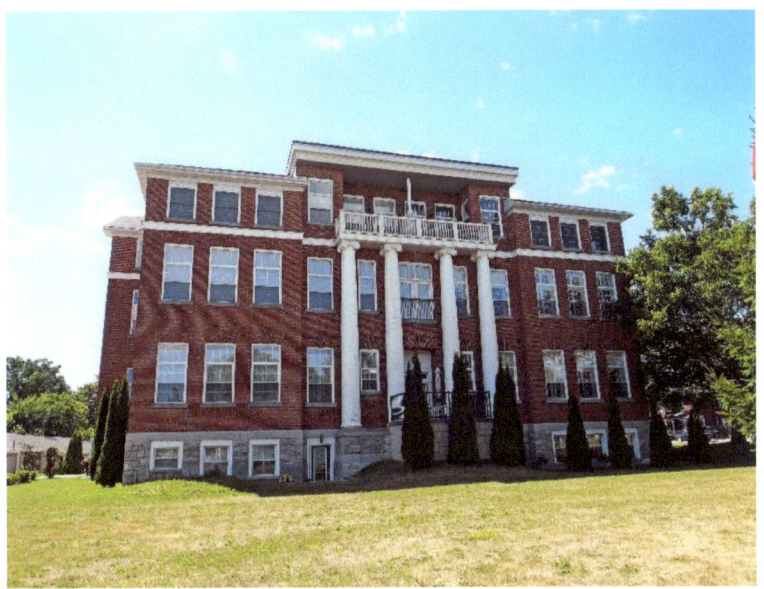

323 George Street – Central School – 1906 - Ionic pillars with balcony above – During the 1990s, the school was closed and converted into the Mansions on George condominiums.

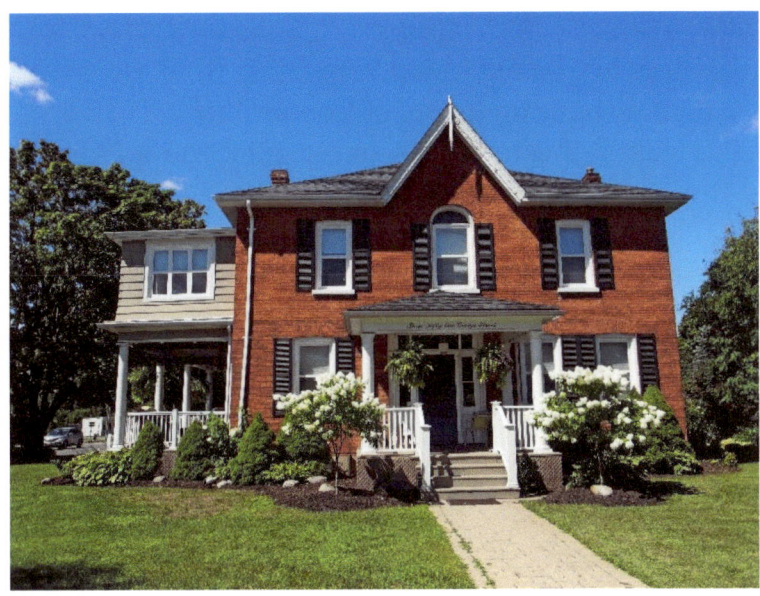

351 George Street

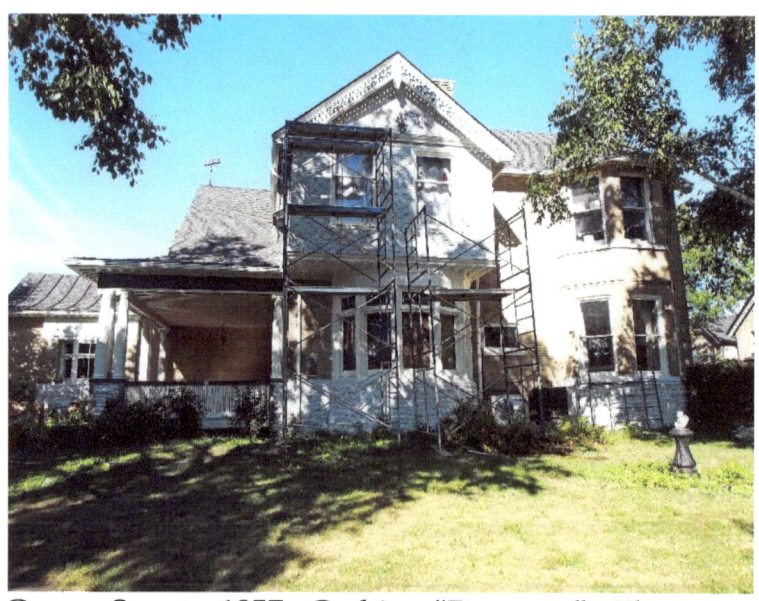

364 George Street – 1857 - Gothic – "Dromore" - Thomas Dumble came to Canada from Cornwall in the early 1840s and made a fortune building many of Cobourg's roads and bridges. He built this residence - steep-pitched roof line, verge board trim on gable, two-storey bay window.

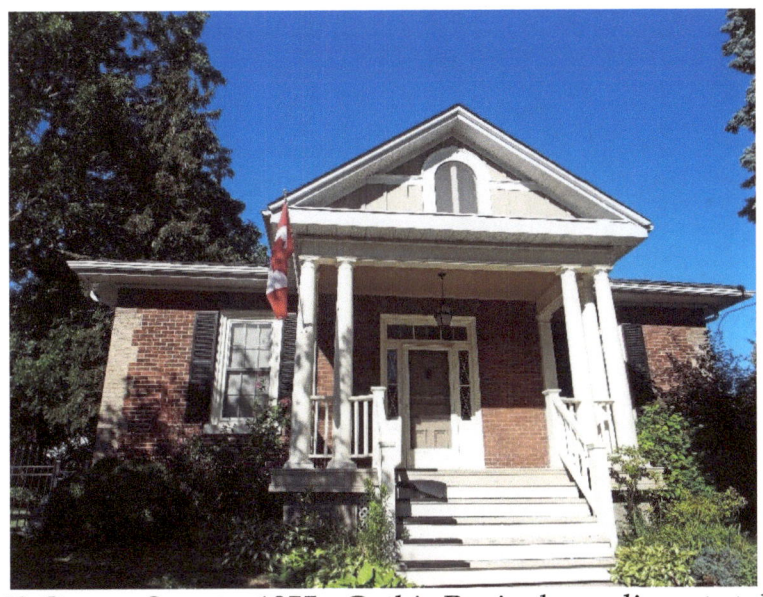

363 George Street – 1855 - Gothic Revival – pediment style porch with slender Tuscan pillars, rectangular sidelights and transom

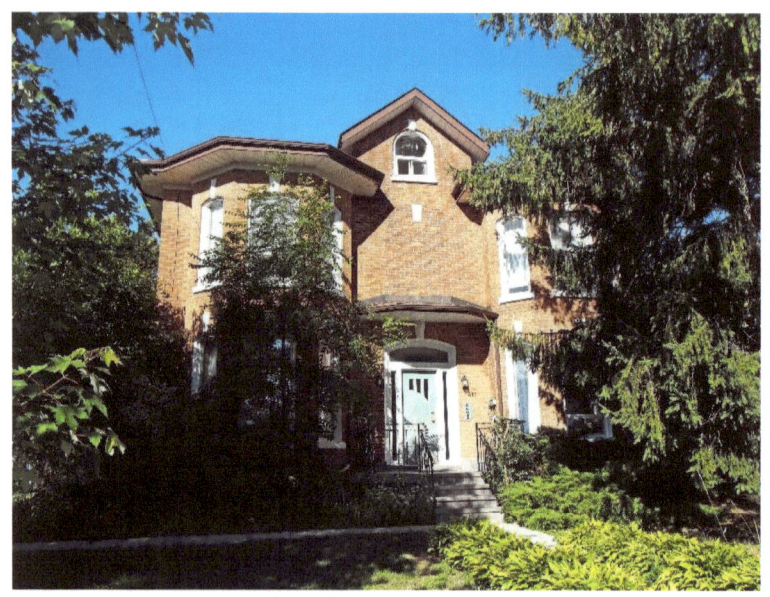

411 George Street

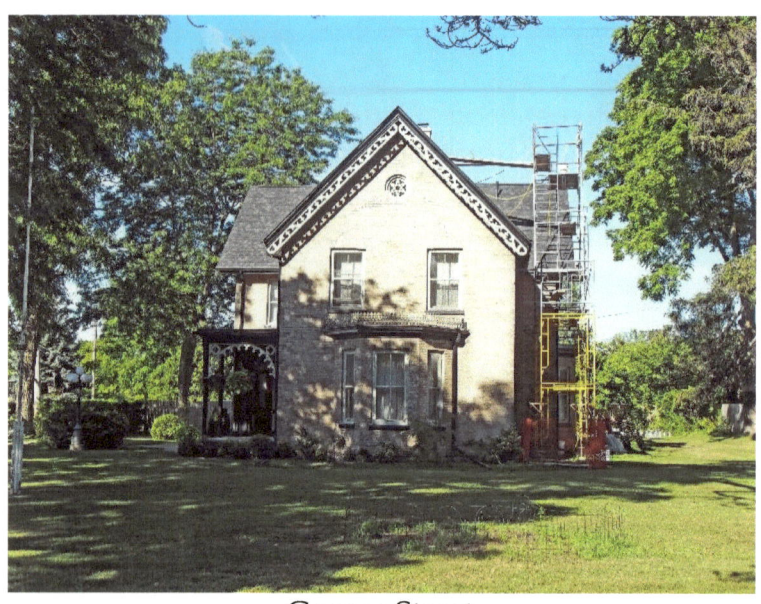

George Street

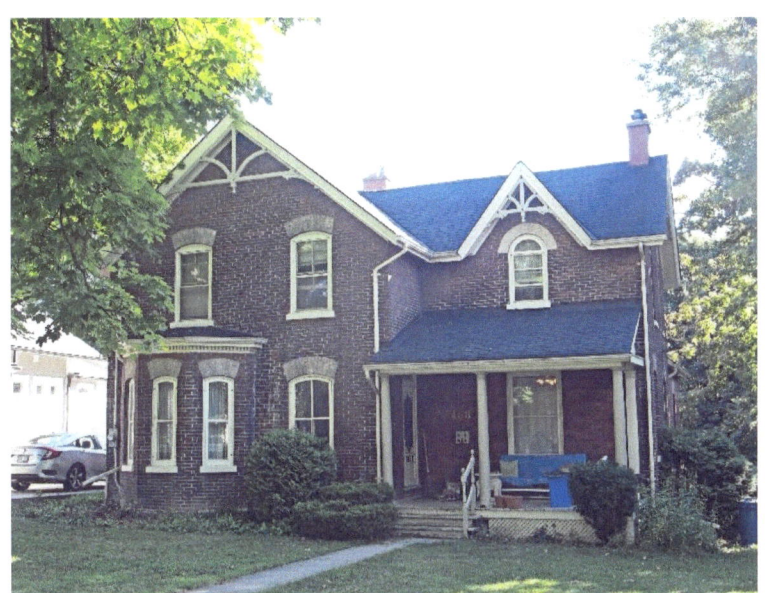

468 George Street

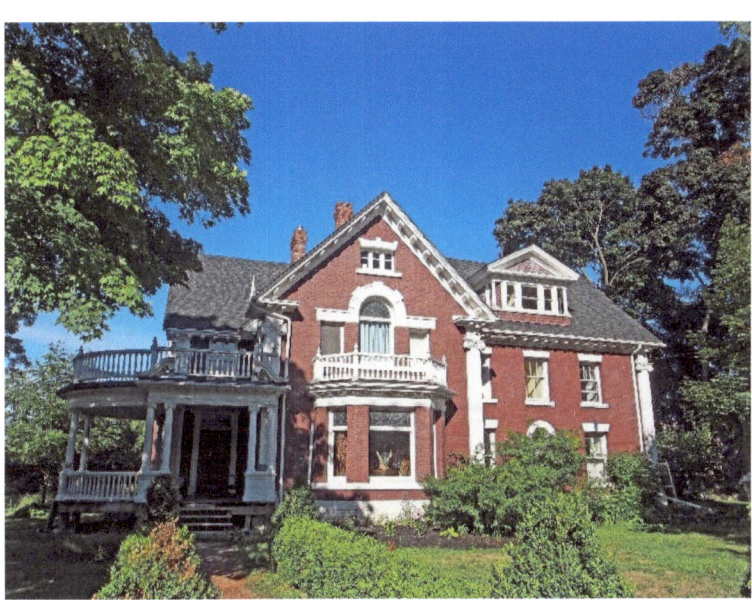

474 George Street – built by Thomas Dumble in 1871 – Gothic
– elaborate front porch added about 1890

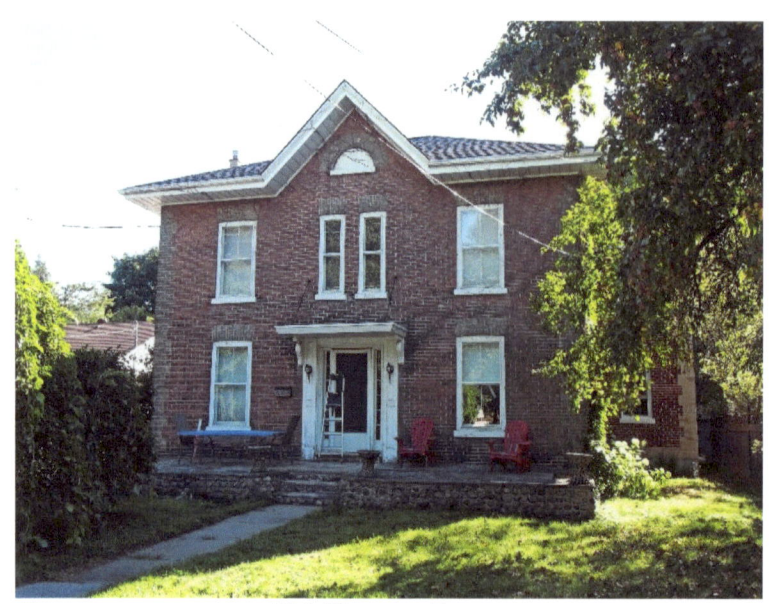

486 George Street

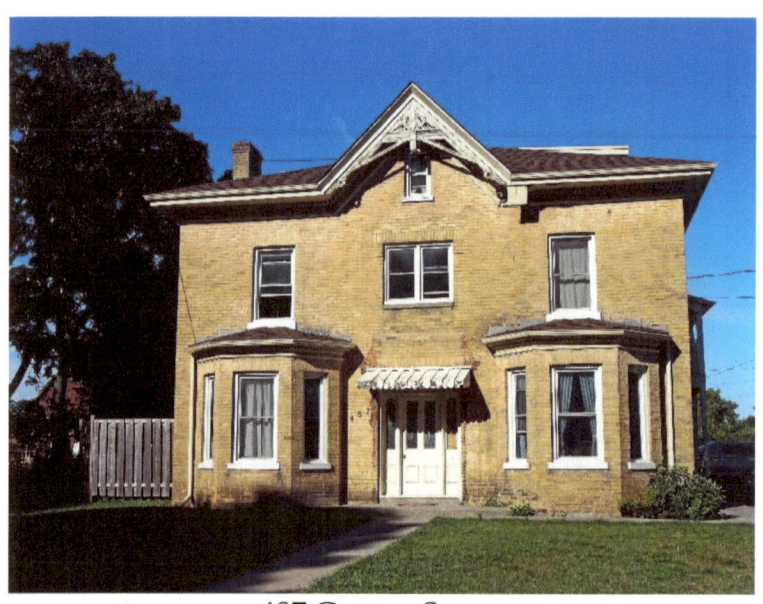

487 George Street

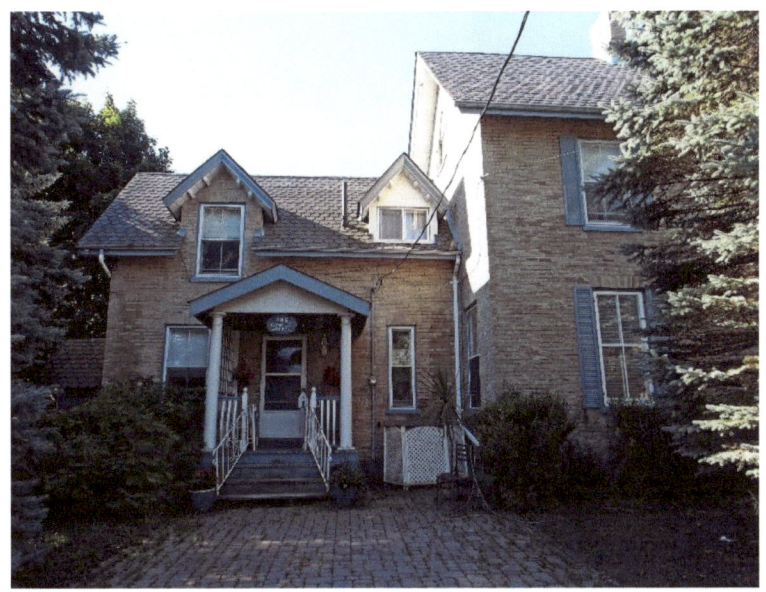

486 George Street

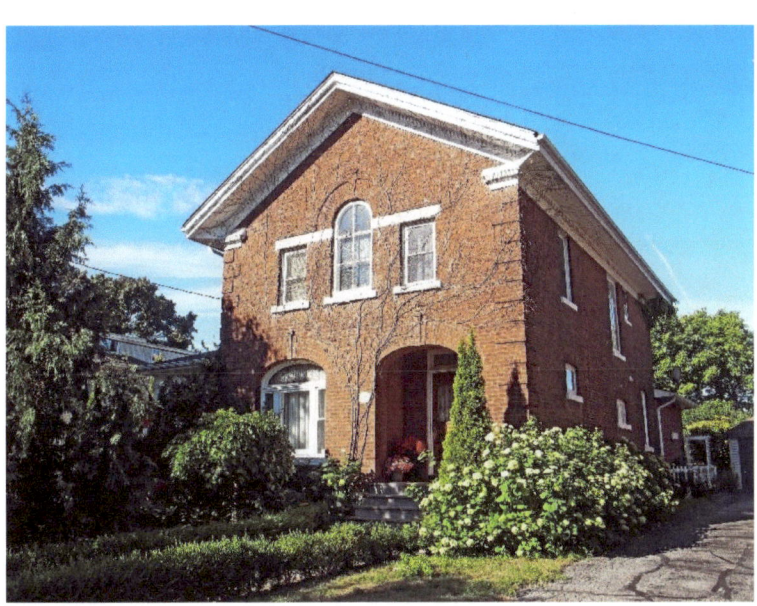

499 George Street

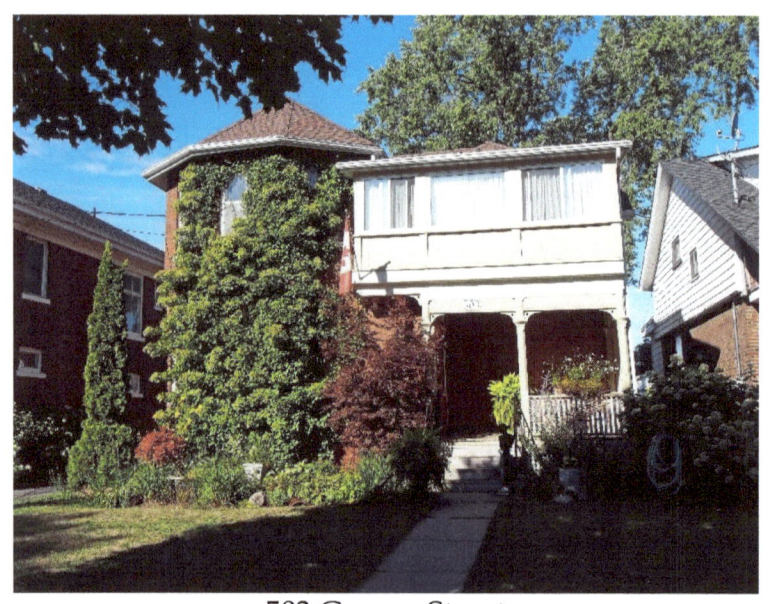

503 George Street

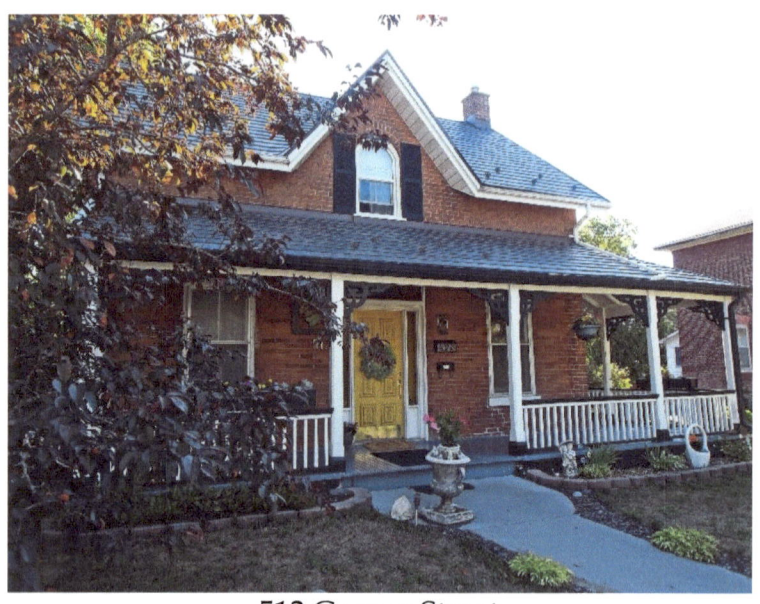

512 George Street

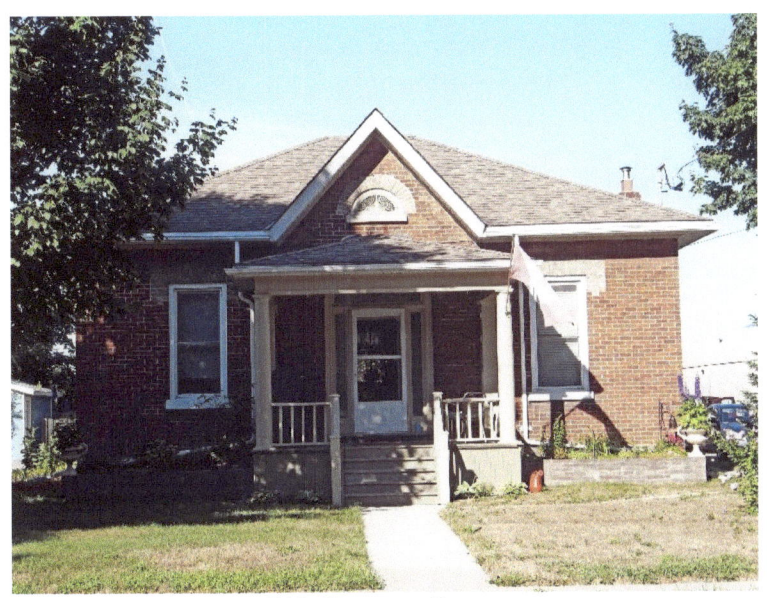

513 George Street

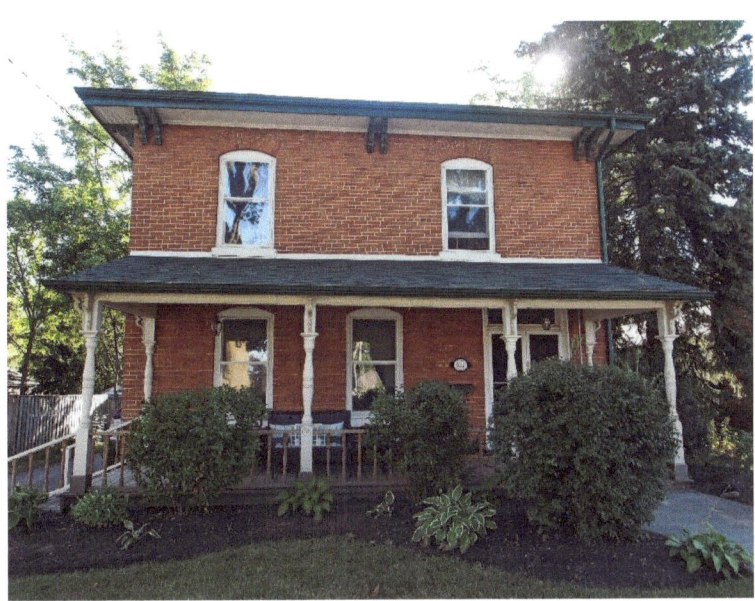

522 George Street

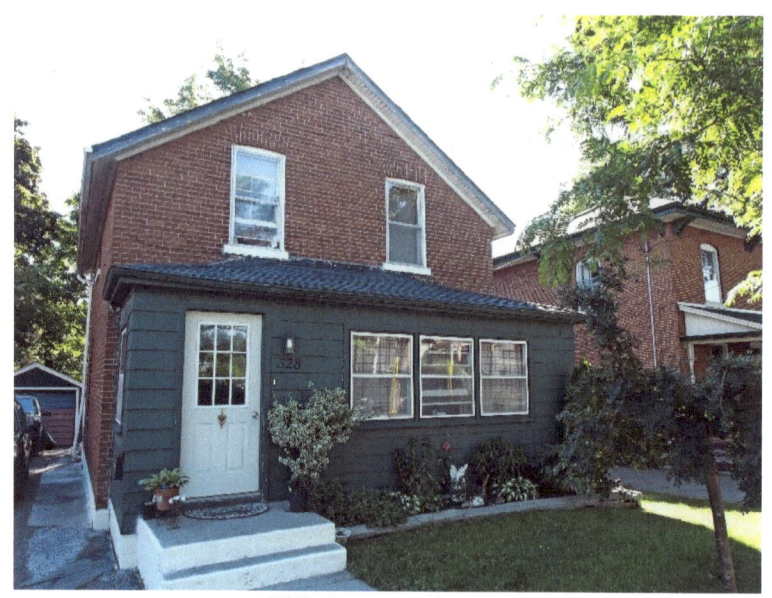

528 George Street

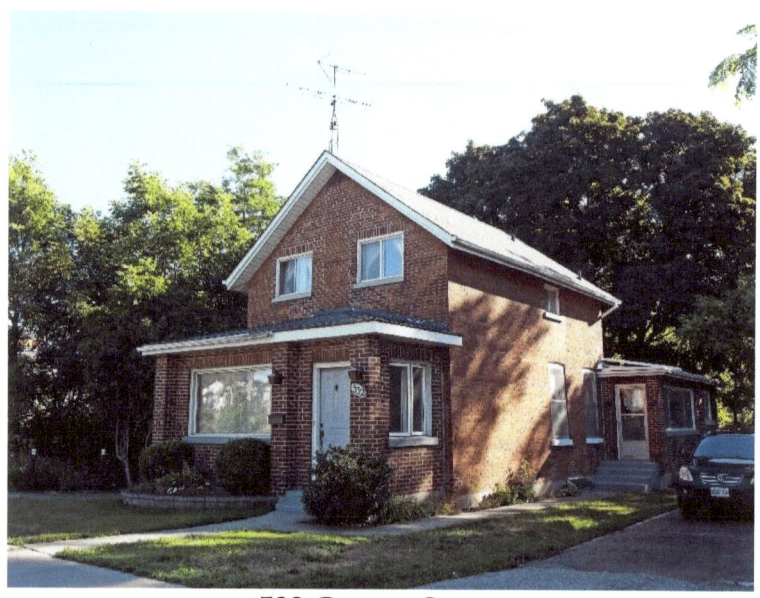

532 George Street

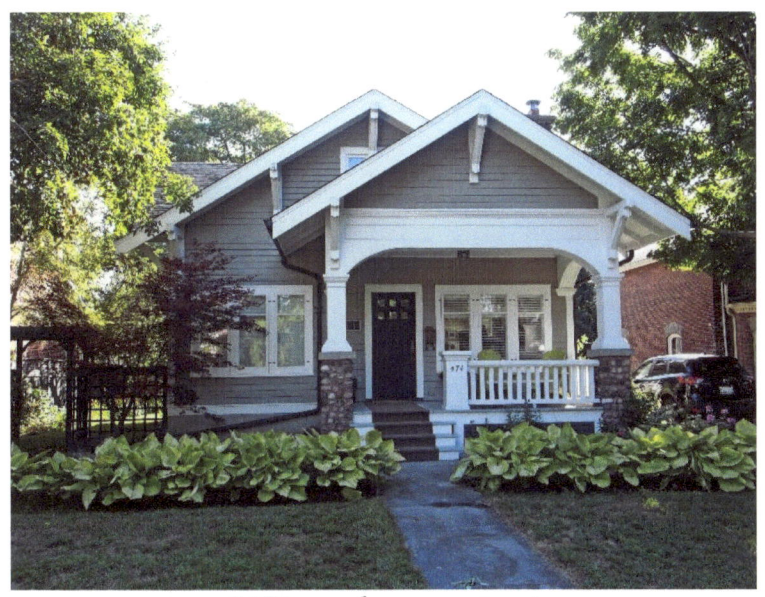

#474 – unknown street

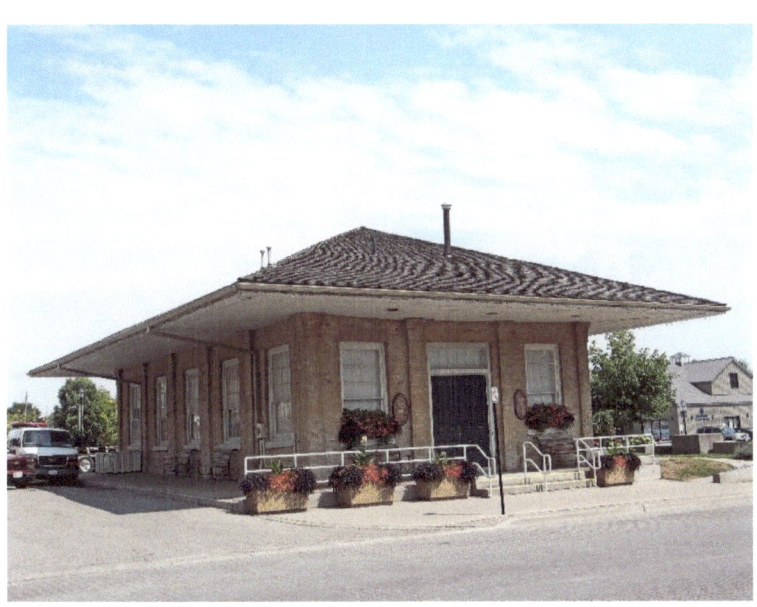

201 Second Street

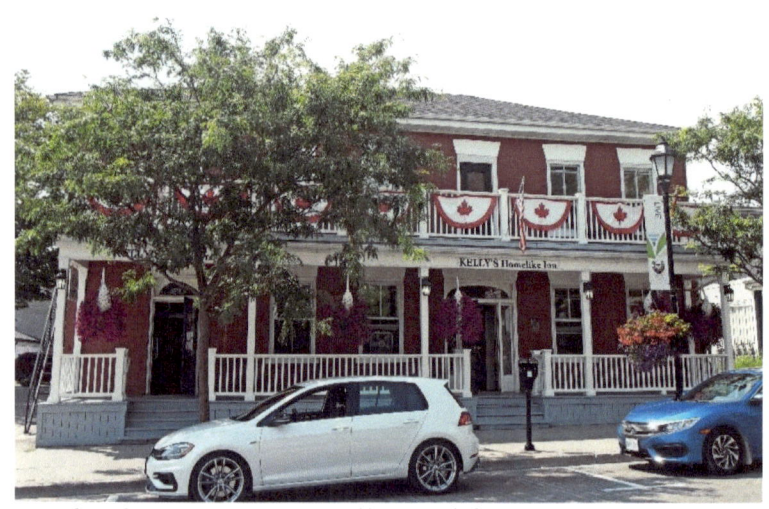

205 Third Street – 1844 – elliptical fan transom over front entrance – "The Homelike Inn"

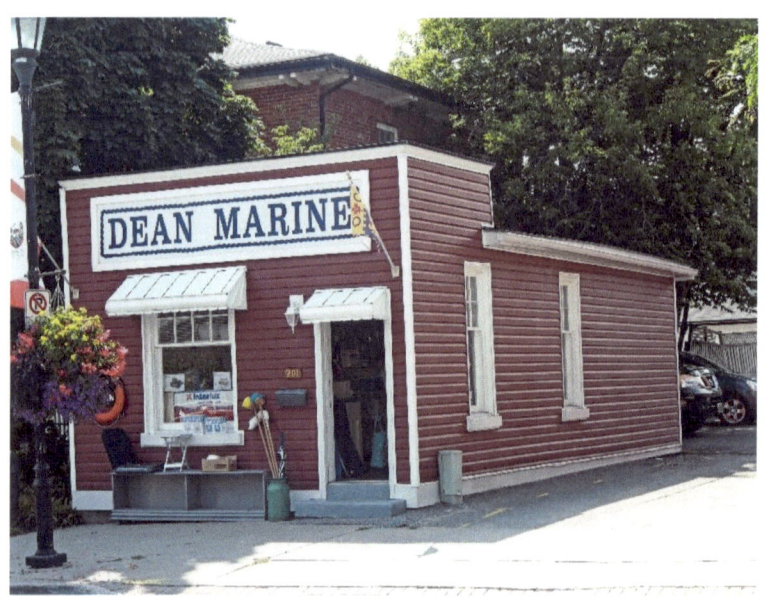

201 Third Street

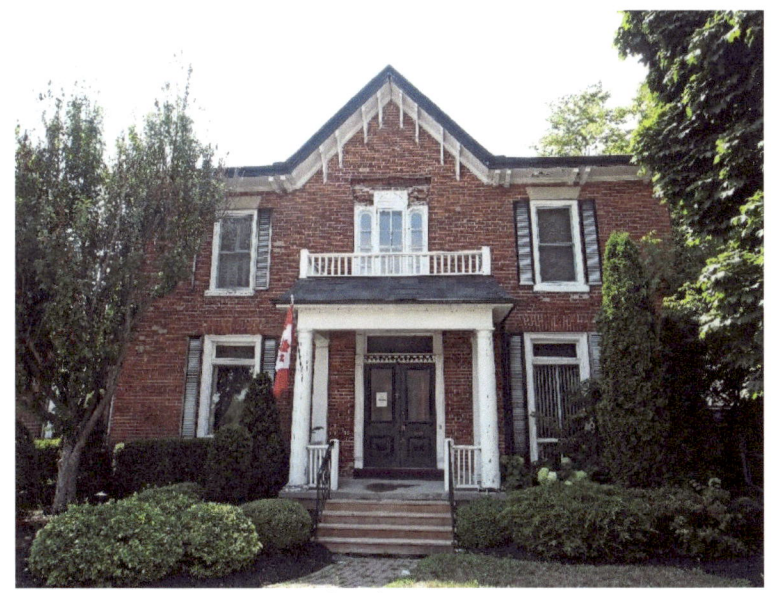

Third Street

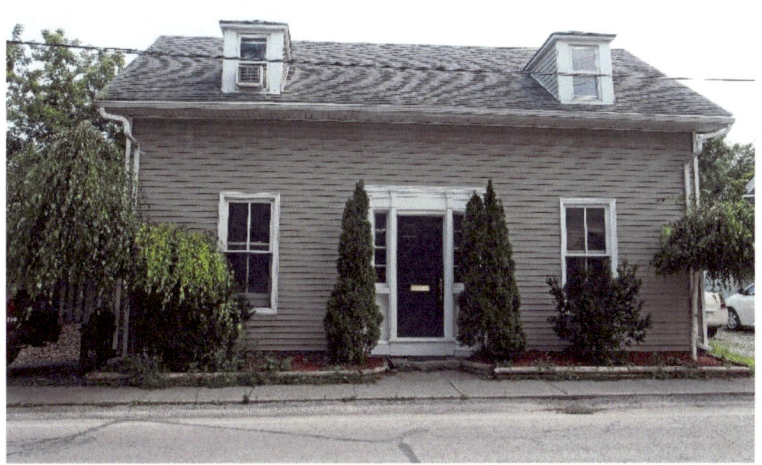

Albert Street

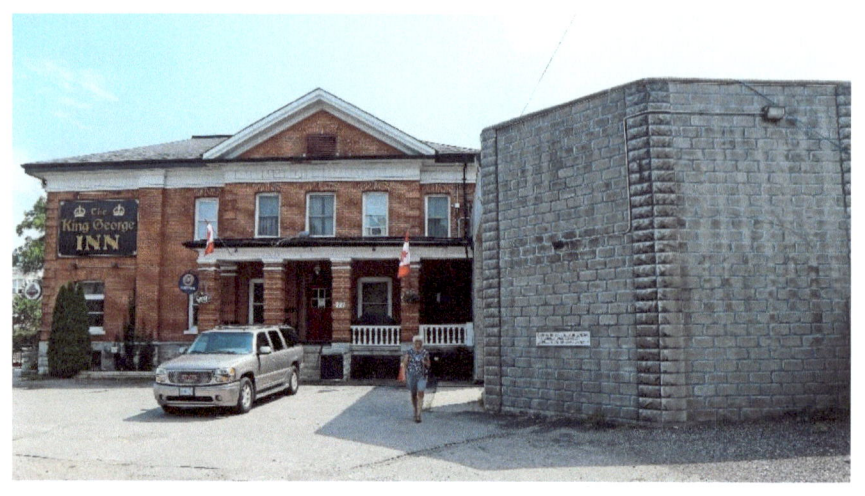

77 Albert Street - Old Cobourg Jail and King George Inn

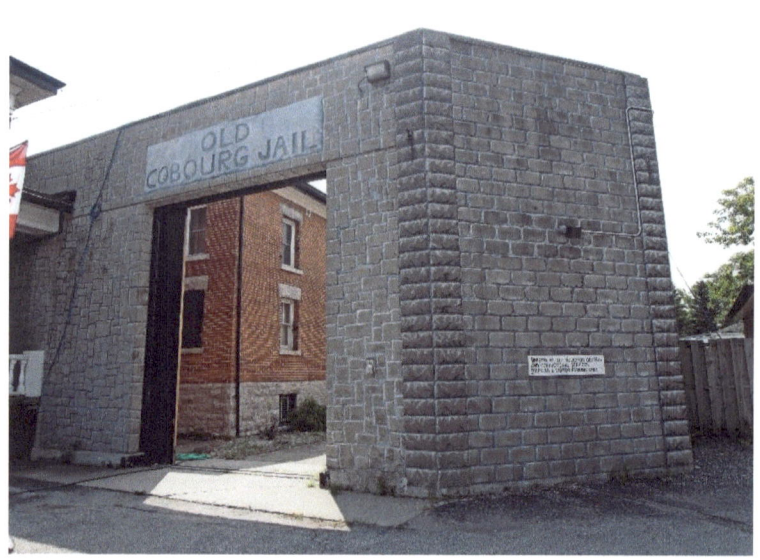

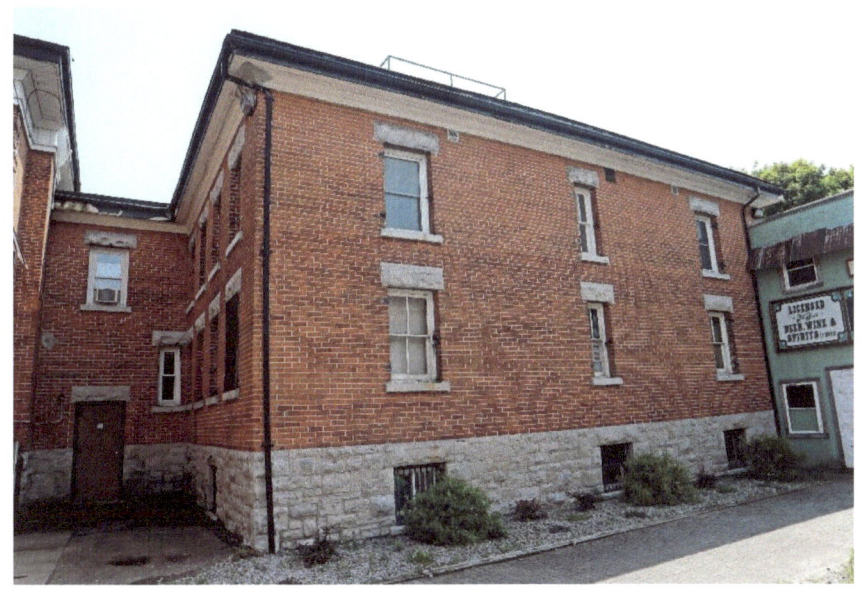

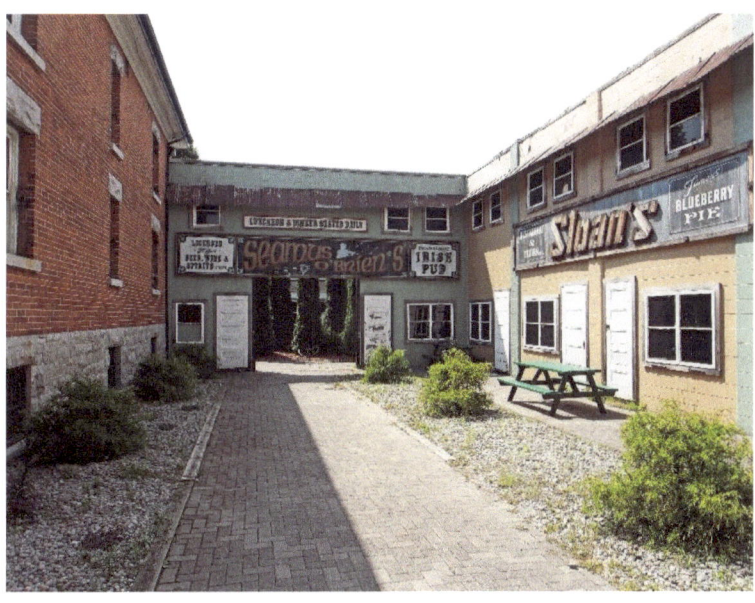

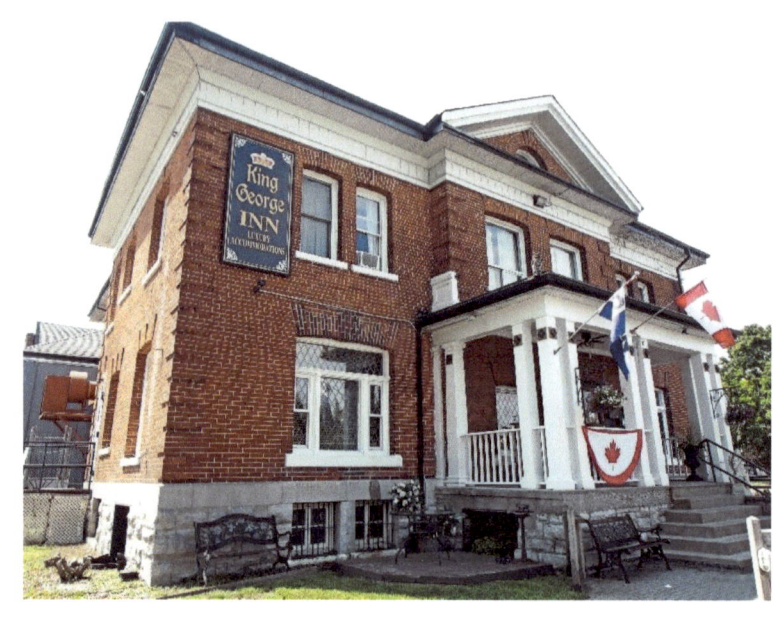

77 Albert Street - King George Inn

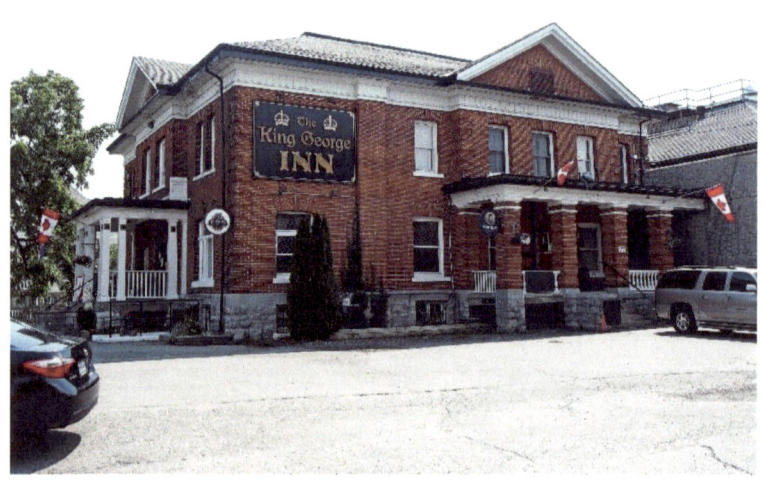

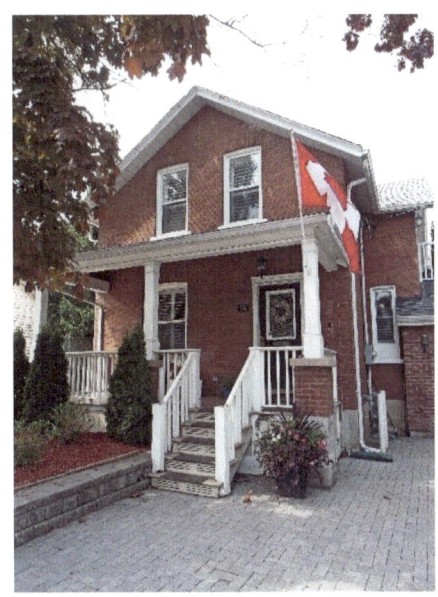

86 Albert Street

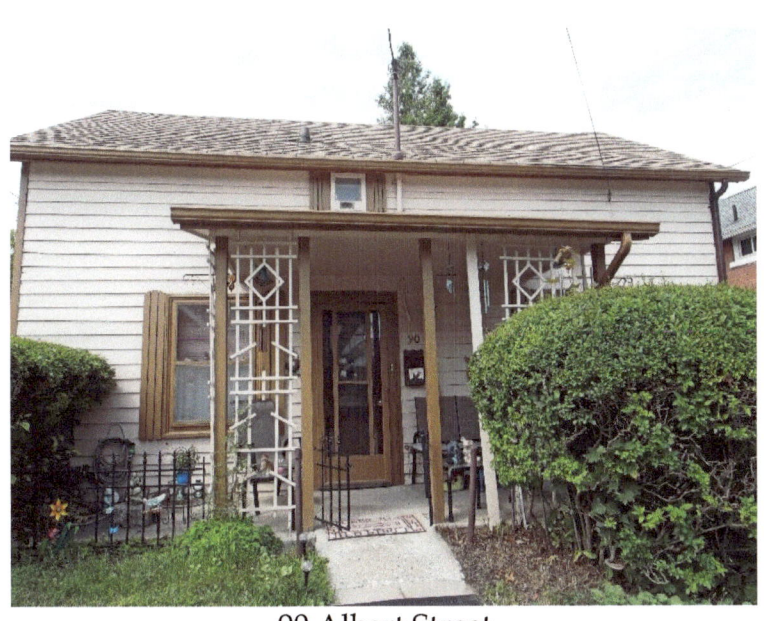

90 Albert Street

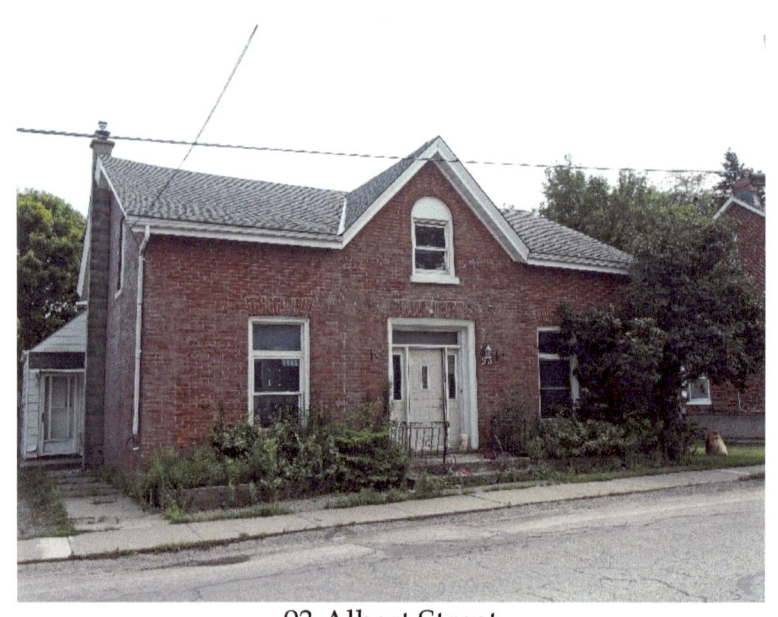

93 Albert Street

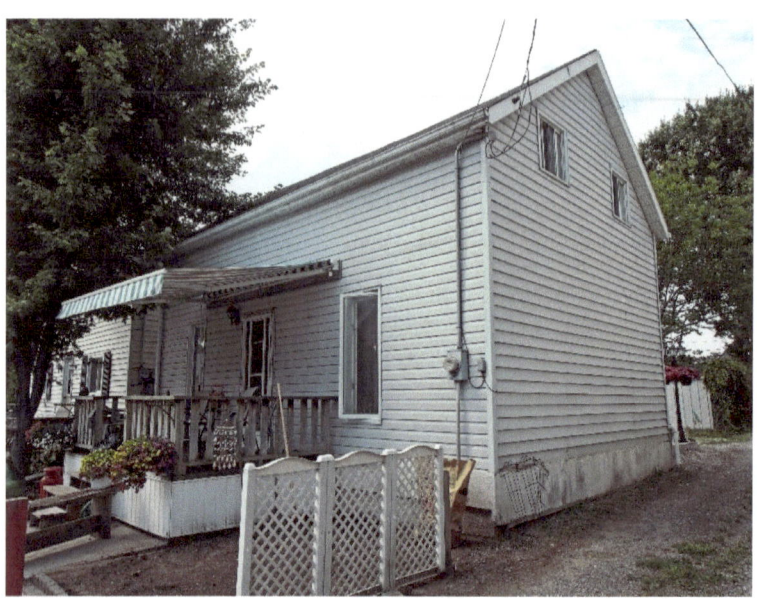

94 Albert Street

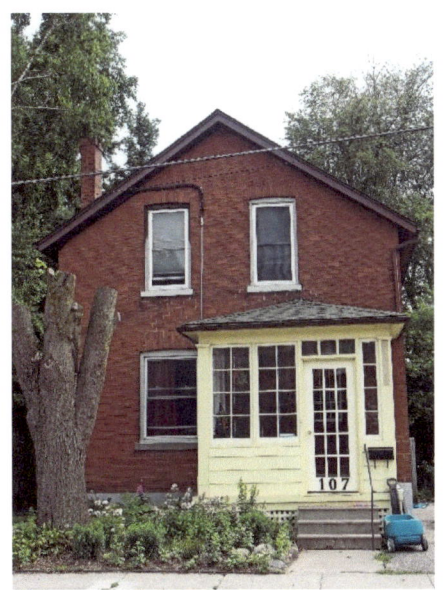

97 Albert Street

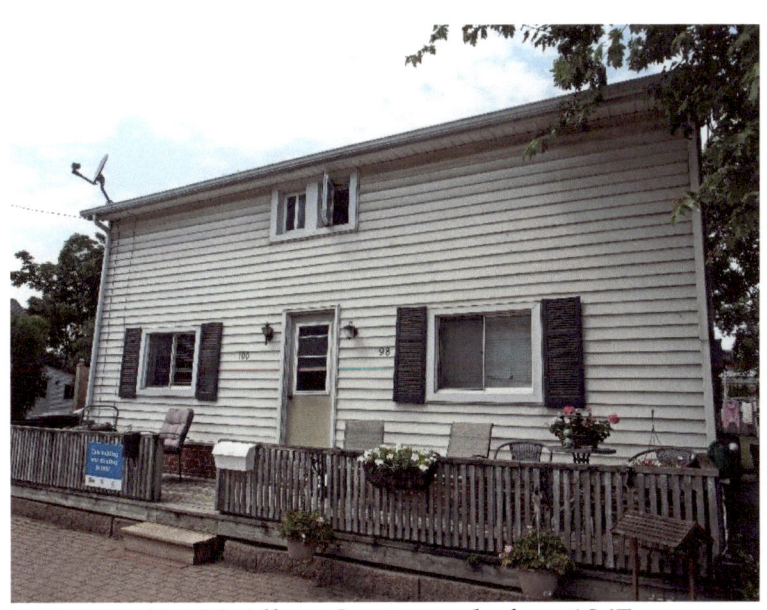

98-100 Albert Street – c. before 1867

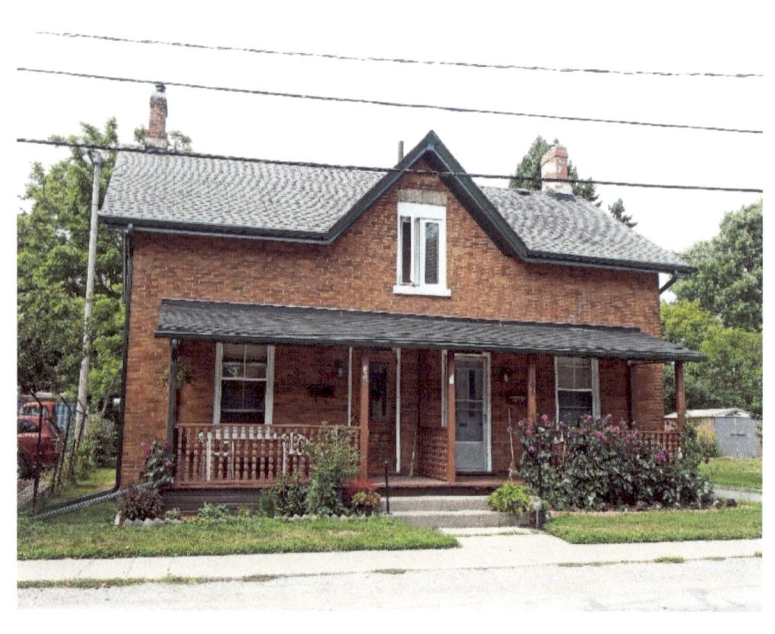

106-108 Albert Street

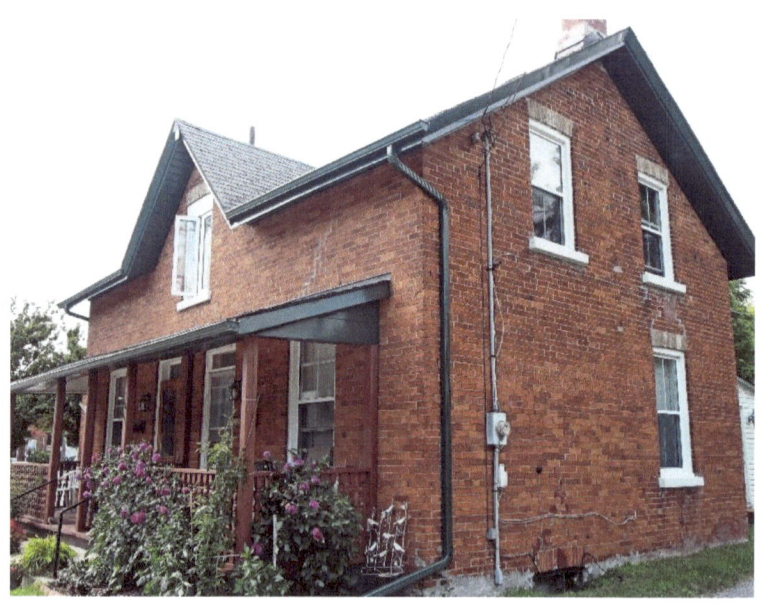

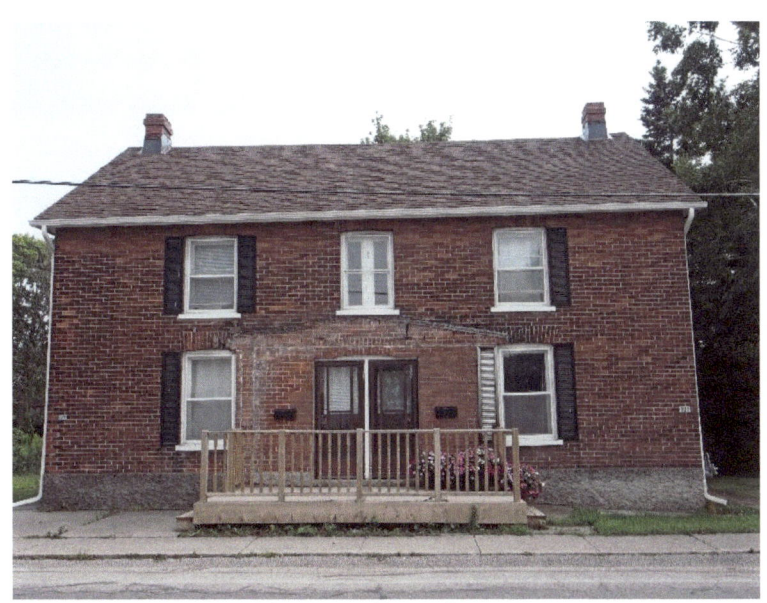

99-101 Albert Street

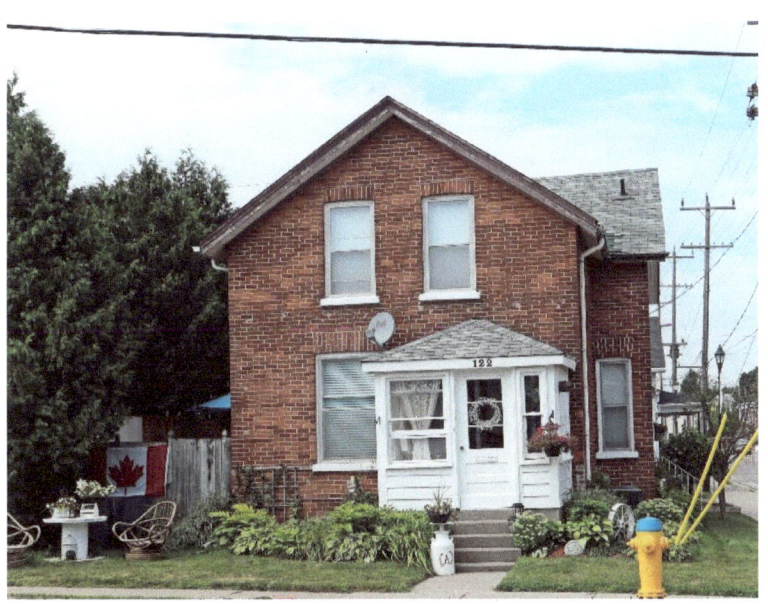

122 Albert Street

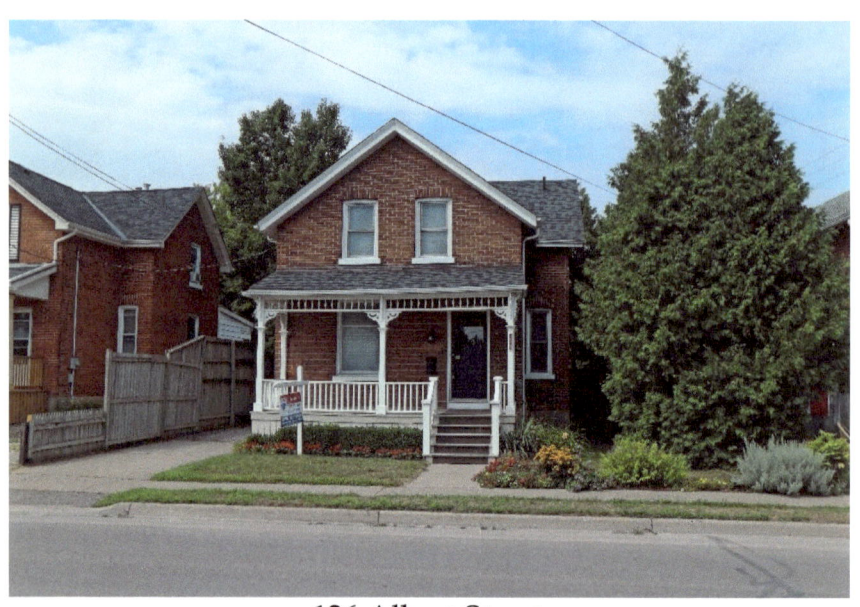

126 Albert Street

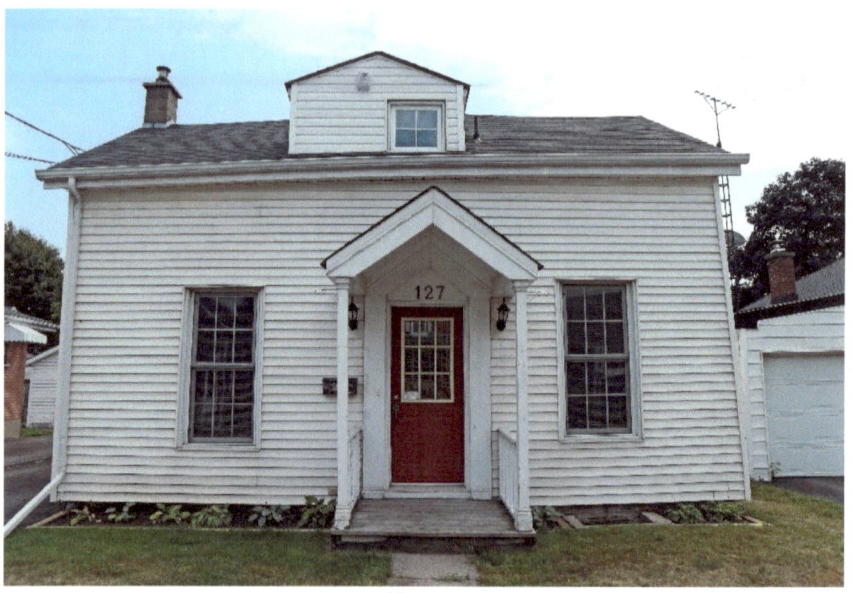

127 Albert Street

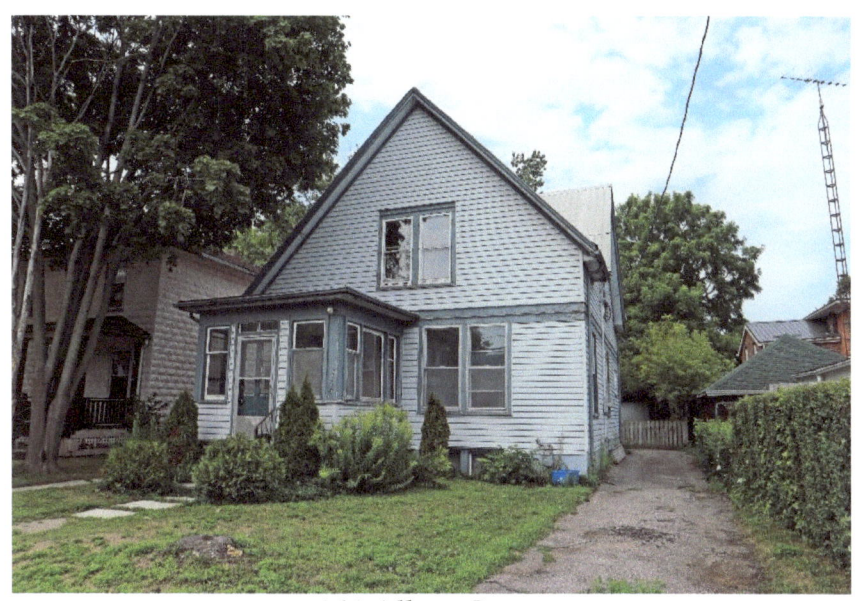

164 Albert Street

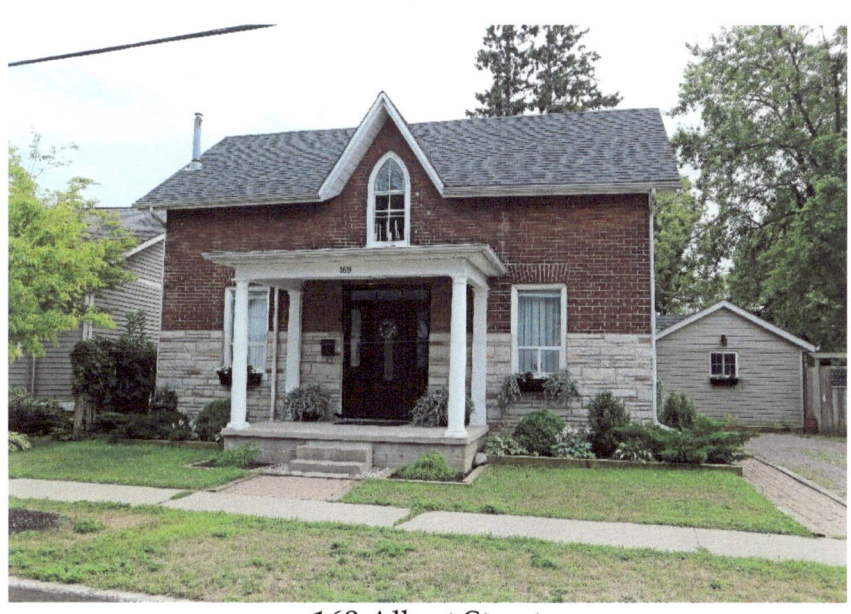

169 Albert Street

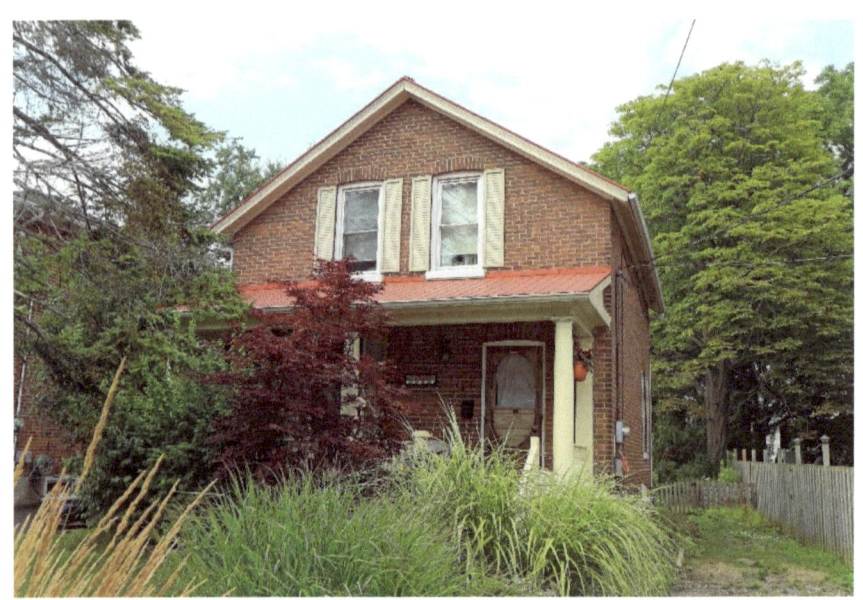

174 Albert Street

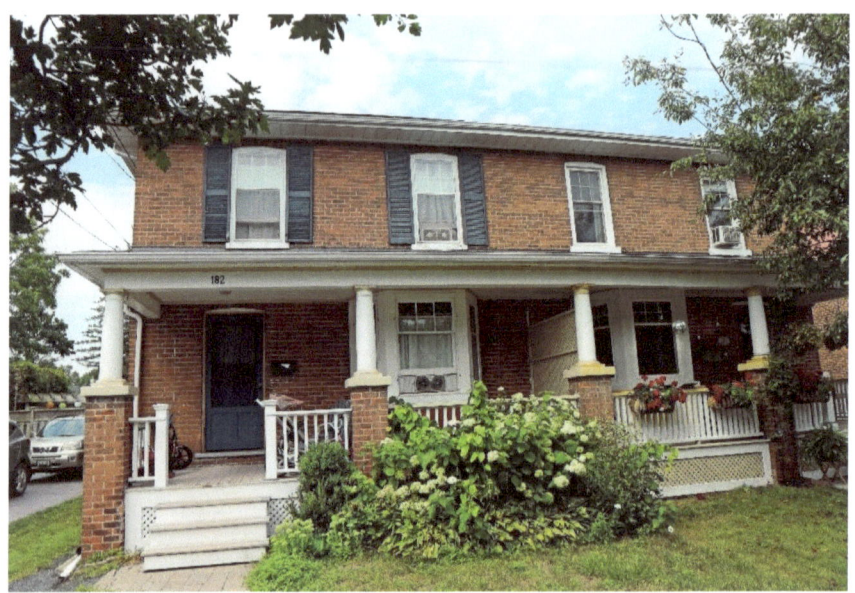

178-182 Albert Street

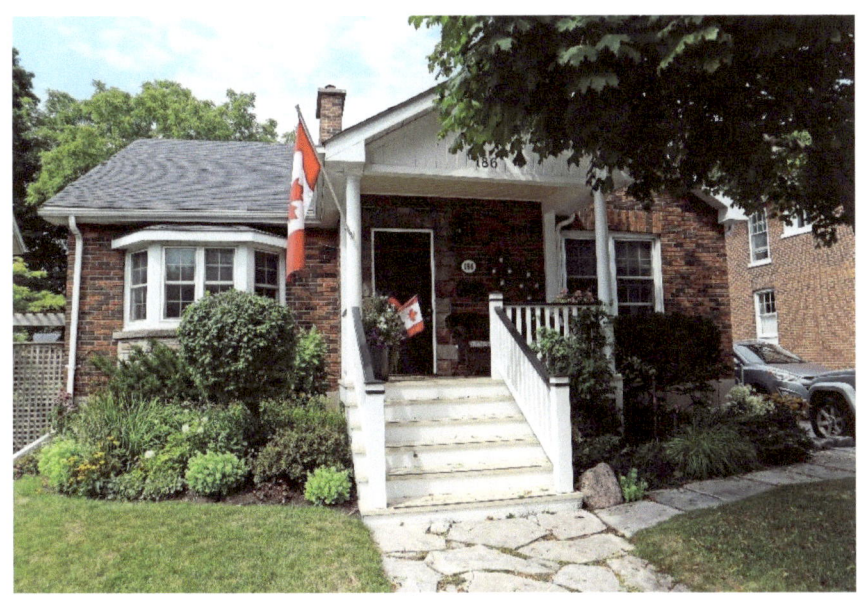

186 Albert Street

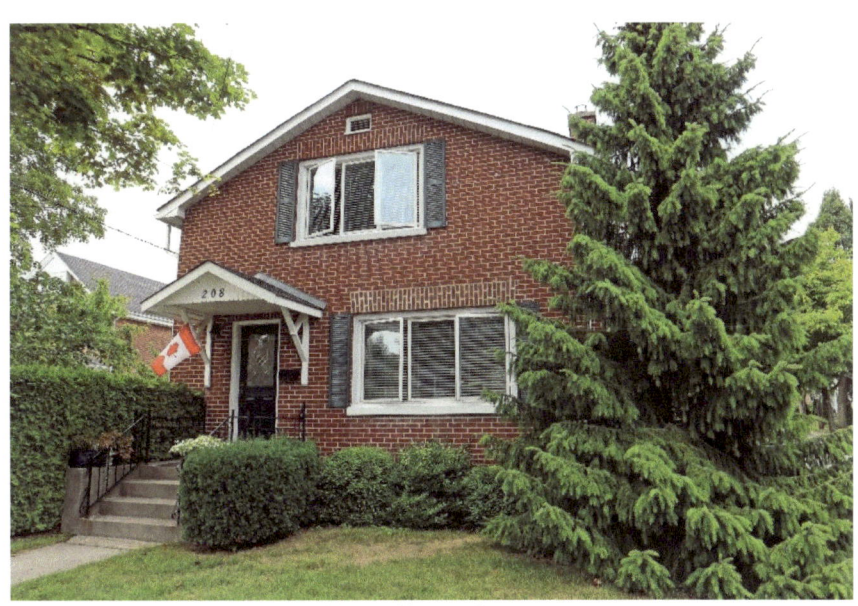

208 Albert Street

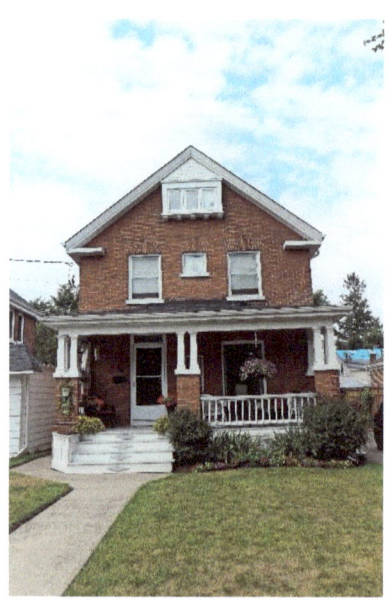

214 Albert Street

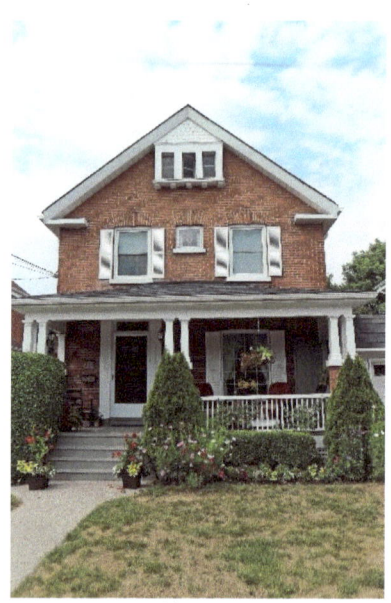

218 Albert Street

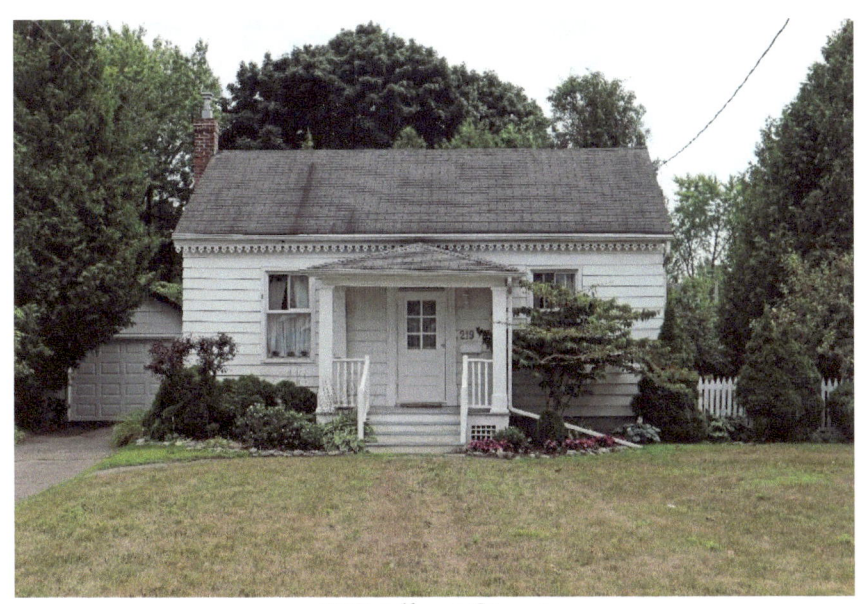

219 Albert Street

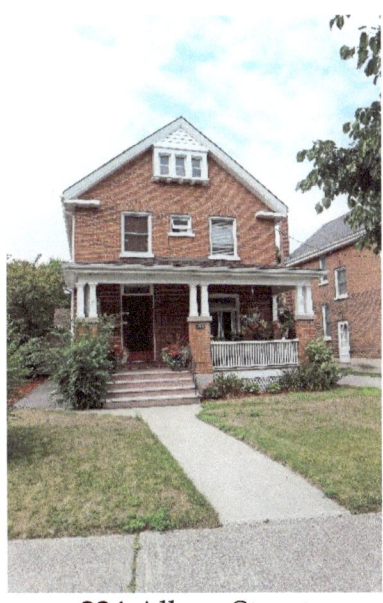

224 Albert Street

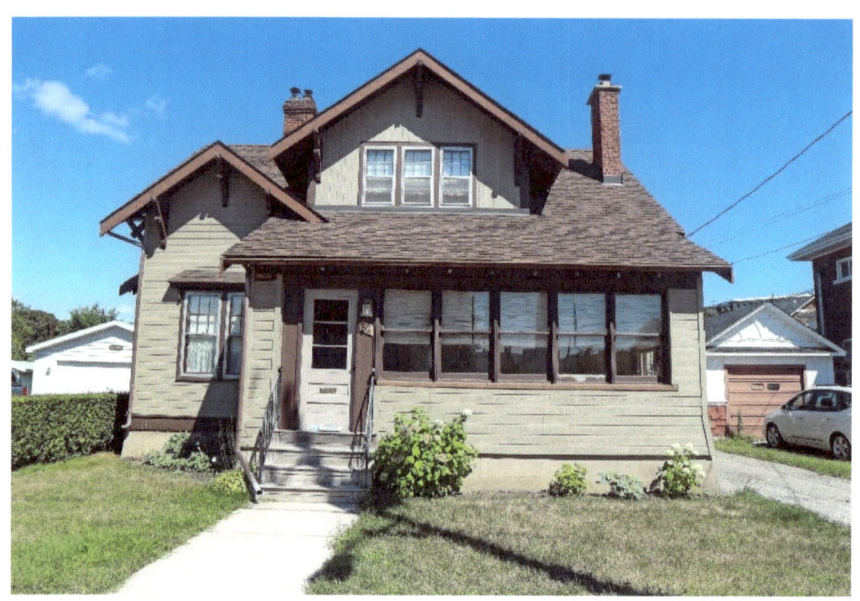

84 Orange Street

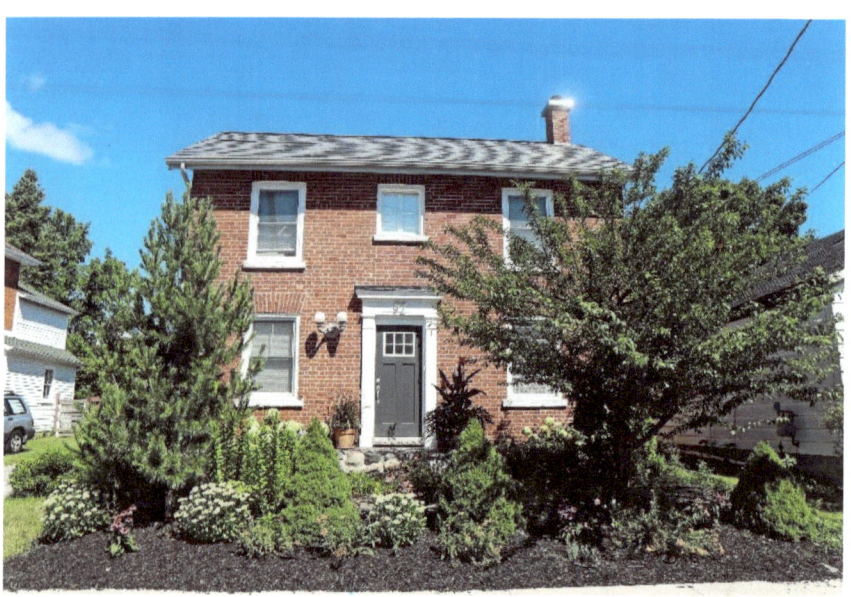

92 Orange Street

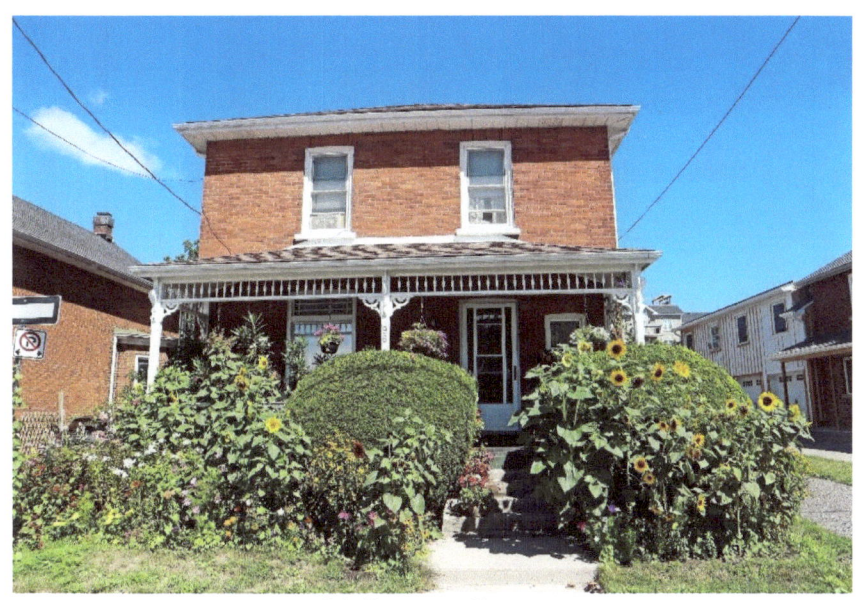
96 Orange Street

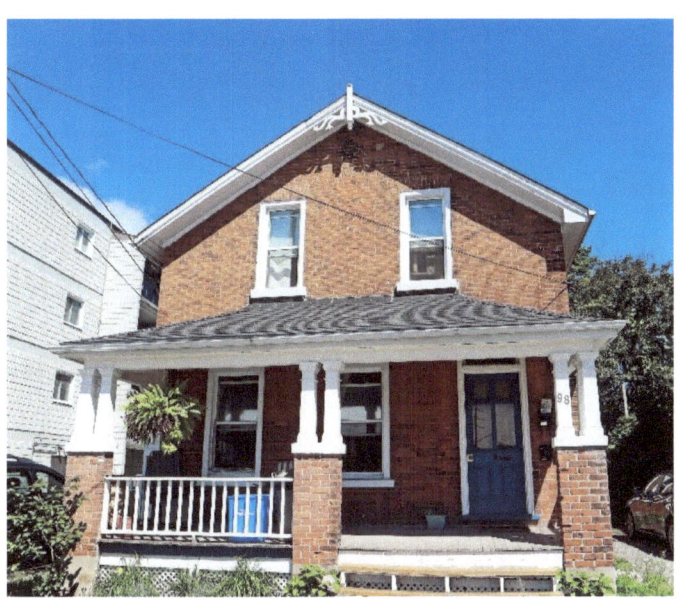
98 Orange Street

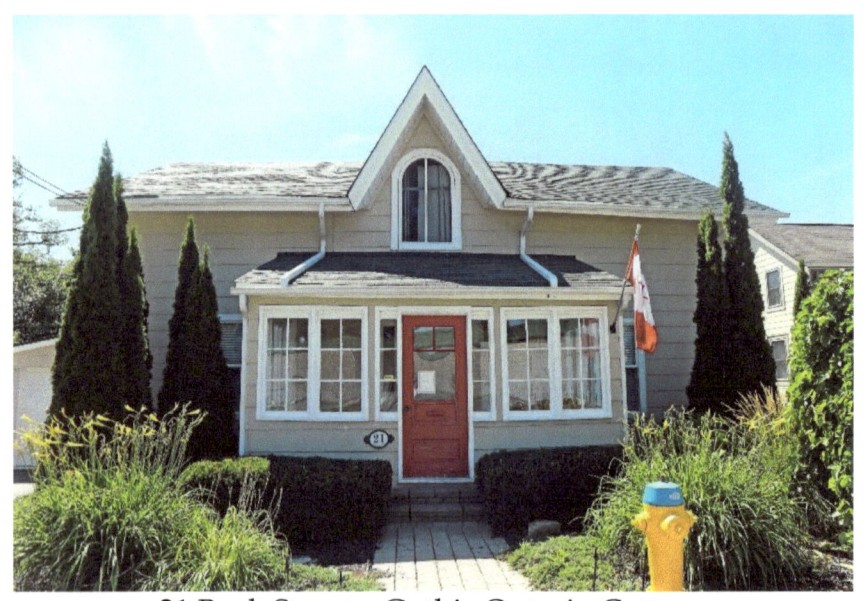

21 Buck Street – Gothic Ontario Cottage

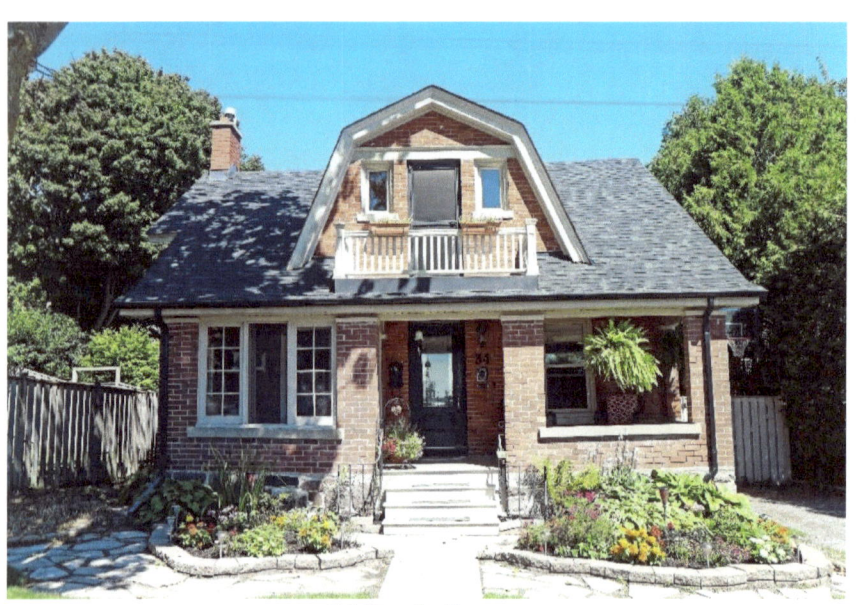

34 Buck Street

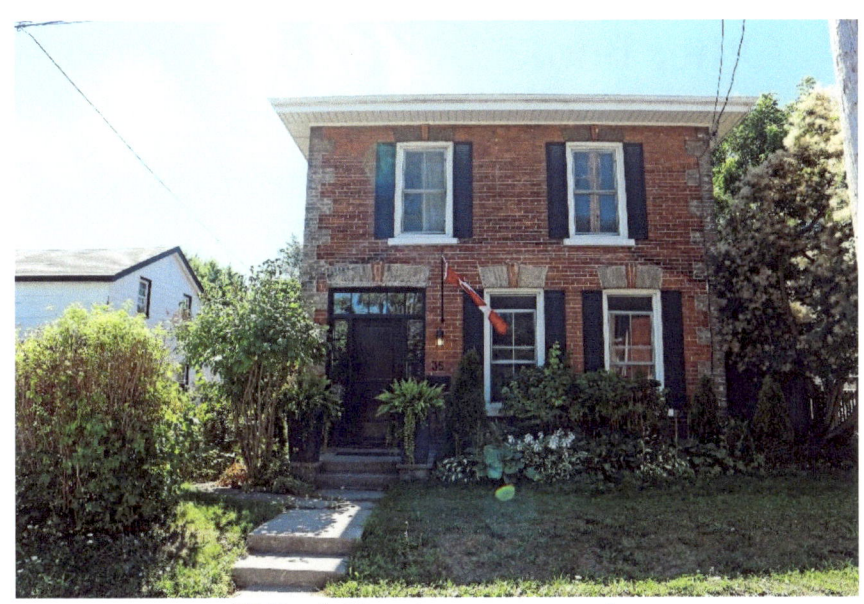

35 Buck Street – corner quoins

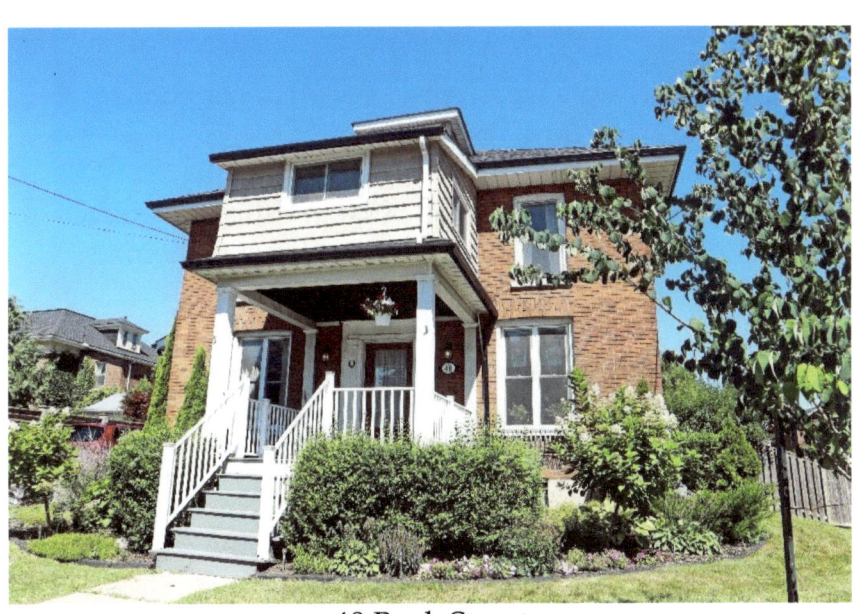

40 Buck Street

Other Books by Barbara Raue

Coins of Gold
Arrows, Indians and Love
The Life and Times of Barbara
The Cromwell Family Book
Laura Secord Discovered
Daddy Where Are You?

Montana Series
Book 1: Montana Dream
Book 2: Life on the Montana Frontier
Book 3: Montana to Boston and Back
Book 4: Montana Sons Go to War
Book 5: Montana Sons Return from War

Visit Barbara's website to view all of her books
http://barbararaue.ca